A Devotional Journey into the Easter Mystery

Also by Christopher Carstens
from Sophia Institute Press:

A Devotional Journey into the Mass
How Mass Can Become a Time of Grace,
Nourishment, and Devotion

CHRISTOPHER CARSTENS

A DEVOTIONAL JOURNEY

INTO THE

EASTER MYSTERY

How Prayerful Participation
in the Paschal Mystery
Brings Life, Joy, and Holiness

Foreword by Dan Burke

SPIRITUAL DIRECTION
SERIES

SOPHIA INSTITUTE PRESS

Manchester, New Hampshire

Sophia Institute Press
Box 5284, Manchester, NH 03108
1-800-888-9344

www.SophiaInstitute.com

Sophia Institute Press® is a registered trademark of Sophia Institute.

Library of Congress Cataloging-in-Publication Data
Names: Carstens, Christopher, 1970- author.
Title: A devotional journey into the Easter mystery : prayful participation in the Paschal mystery brings life, joy, and holiness / Christopher Carstens ; foreword by Dan Burke.
Description: Manchester, New Hampshire : Sophia Institute Press, 2020. | Series: Spiritual direction series | Includes bibliographical references. | Summary: "How to enter into the mystery of Easter through the Catholic liturgy"— Provided by publisher.
Identifiers: LCCN 2019049712 | ISBN 9781622826629 (paperback) | ISBN 9781622826629 (ebook)
Subjects: LCSH: Holy Week. | Paschal mystery. | Catholic Church—Liturgy. | Catholic Church—Doctrines.
Classification: LCC BV90 .C365 2020 | DDC 264/.02—dc23
LC record available at https://lccn.loc.gov/2019049712

First printing

Contents

APPENDICES

Lifting the Veil on the Easter Mystery

✠

For everything created by God is good, and noth-
ing is to be rejected when received with thanksgiving, for
it is made holy by the invocation of God in prayer.

—1 Timothy 4:4–5

The human person was designed by God to recognize and seek patterns—harmony. This is why we love music and melody. Like God, we can truly see beauty, and see that it is good. Indeed, these beautiful patterns connect to the deepest part of who we are, because in that deepest place, God dwells as the author of music and melody. He dwells in a heavenly symphony—a sacred dance of peace, healing, and divine life. Saints know this sacred rhythm and without exception have entered into it and have given themselves over to it completely. This is why they are saints. When God leads, they follow in the dance of the Bridegroom. They become saints when they follow without effort because, though distinct in nature, they are one in will. Because we are all called to be saints, to know and live in this sacred rhythm, we are thereby called to enter into the melody of God. This is why He has brought us into existence.

Where is this melody, and how can we find our place in it? The answer is simple and complex. The melody is found in the rhythm of the sacraments and the liturgical seasons. A lifelong Catholic who exists in the context of a banal liturgical experience of the postconciliar Mass might shrug his shoulders at this with wonder. "What's the big deal?" At the same time, the saint sees the liturgy as a big deal because in the divine rhythm, the divine life is waiting to be known and to burst into his soul to change him — and the world. The reason cradle Catholics might shrug their shoulders is that they have been robbed, for reasons outside the scope of this book, of the vision of God in the liturgy.

Yet this book, A Devotional Journey into the Easter Mystery — like all the liturgical writings of Christopher Carstens — seeks to draw back the veil that has hidden the melody of God from our generation. Carstens leads us, as into the most beautiful but abandoned room in an ancient, majestic castle, into the throne room of grace, where the angels sing and the heart is lifted to the glory of the Blessed Trinity.

Give your heart to this work, give your heart to the liturgy of God, and you will find the God of the liturgy in ways you never thought possible.

Let the journey begin!

— Dan Burke

A Devotional Journey
into the Easter Mystery

Introduction

✠

Have you ever wondered what God was doing *before* He made heaven and earth? If you have, you are not alone. But you should know that, at least according to one ancient thinker, such a pondering is not without its dangers. As St. Augustine (d. 430) recalls, to the question "What was God doing before creation," one wiseacre quipped, "He was making hells for those who pry into such deep matters!"[1]

The questions of time—what it is, when (and if) it began, and where it goes—are not easy to grasp, and questions of eternity are nearly impossible to answer. Why else did St. Augustine's head spin in contemplating what God was up to during that "time" before creation? Yet, time stands as a key symbol in our understanding and celebration of the Catholic liturgy—and especially the high point of the Catholic liturgy: the Easter Mystery. For example, Easter celebrates the saving work of Jesus at a particular *time of the year*: the first Sunday after the first full moon following the spring equinox. Its mystery unfolds through specific *days of the week*: Ash Wednesday, Palm Sunday, Holy

---

[1]   See *Confessions*, XI, 12, translated by F. J. Sheed (New York: Sheed and Ward, 1943), 269.

Thursday, Good Friday, Holy Saturday. It also associates itself with certain *times of the day*: the Mass of the Lord's Supper takes place "in the evening,"[2] Good Friday's liturgical observance of the Passion begins about three o'clock in the afternoon,[3] and the Paschal Vigil "must take place during the night," even after midnight.[4] Even though Christ's saving work exists eternally before God the Father, its liturgical observance is time-bound for us here and now.

Observing correct time is thus a necessary first step to entering into the Easter Mystery. But time isn't simply a question to be pondered by philosophers such as St. Augustine and his smart-aleck interlocutor. Time, as slippery as it may seem, finds tangible expression in human calendars. Julius Caesar gave a great start to our Western world (and beyond) when he established a new calendar back in 45 B.C. According to the Julian calendar's reckoning, each natural year accounted 365 days and 6 hours for the earth to orbit the sun. Thus, for three years, the calendar year was 365 days long, and every fourth year the accumulating hours added another day, 366 days (added as February 29). Apparently, though, allotting 365 days and 6 hours was not quite exact enough: in fact, the total time for earth's orbit is closer to 365 days, 5 hours, and 49 minutes. And while 11 minutes per year may

---

[2] Roman Missal (Washington, D.C.: USCCB Publishing, 2011), Thursday of the Lord's Supper, no. 1.

[3] Roman Missal, Friday of the Passion of the Lord, no. 4.

[4] Roman Missal, Easter Vigil in the Holy Night, nos. 3–4. The Holy See's 1988 Circular Letter "Concerning the Preparation and Celebration of the Easter Feasts" (*Paschalis Sollemnitatis*) even goes on to call "reprehensible" those practices "whereby the Easter Vigil is celebrated at the time of day that it is customary to celebrate anticipated Sunday Masses" (78).

not seem like much, over the course of the centuries—sixteen of them, to be precise—these annual 11-minute discrepancies turned into a nearly 11-day difference! In the early sixteenth century, for example, while the man-made calendar read June 22 and should have been the longest day of the year, the solar or natural calendar—since it had been running faster than Julius Caesar's calendar—had already spilled into July.

To bring man's time back into alignment with nature's time —and, for our purposes, God's liturgical time—Pope Gregory XIII (d. 1585) implemented a new system for orienting calendar time with cosmic time.[5] He also decreed that the 11-day lag be made up at once: October 4, 1582, was followed the next day by October 15, 1582. Thus, by papal decree, the world lost ten calendar days! What's more, the Doctor of the Church St. Teresa of Jesus died after midnight on what should have been October 5, 1582. For this reason, today her feast day is celebrated on October 15.

Natural time, though, is not the only measure of the mystery of Easter. Even though grace presupposes nature, supernatural time must also take its bearings between the Alpha and the Omega. Yet here, too, the sacred timepiece had slipped a cog or two over the years.

In the earliest centuries of the Church, the liturgies of the Paschal Triduum[6] were celebrated at times associated with the

---

[5] According to the United States Naval Observatory, "Every year that is exactly divisible by four is a leap year, except for years that are exactly divisible by 100, but these centurial years are leap years if they are exactly divisible by 400. For example, the years 1700, 1800, and 1900 are not leap years, but the year 2000 is."

[6] *Triduum* means "three days" and indicates the period beginning with the Mass of the Lord's Supper on Holy Thursday evening and concluding with Vespers (Evening Prayer) on Easter Sunday.

historical realities that they in some way made present: the Mass of the Lord's Supper on the evening of Holy Thursday, the Passion of Jesus on the afternoon of Good Friday, and the Resurrection of Christ during the night between Holy Saturday and Easter Sunday morning. These moments in the Paschal liturgies, however, soon began to experience mission creep as the clergy and the faithful began to drift away from the original liturgical time slots, a point that the Vatican noted when it reformed the Easter liturgy in the 1950s: "During the middles ages they began, for various pertinent reasons, to set an earlier time for the performance of liturgical services on those days, so that toward the end of that period all of these liturgical services had been transferred to the morning. This did not take place without detriment to the liturgical meaning."[7]

A renowned priest and pastor who worked in the Archdiocese of Saint Louis, Father Martin Hellriegel (1890–1981), described his parish's celebration of Holy Thursday in the 1940s: "We distributed holy Communion on Holy Thursday every half hour between six and seven-thirty [in the morning], the high Mass being at eight [a.m.].... Furthermore, the greater part of the congregation, particularly the adults, were left *without* holy Mass on the very day of its birthday anniversary. Therefore, we decided to transfer the solemn high Mass to 5:50 a.m., with the result that by far the greater part of the parish, the children included, are now at this great eucharistic-family-celebration."[8] (I don't

---

[7] Sacred Congregation of Rites, Decree on the Restoration of the Holy Week Order *Maxima redemptionis nostrae mysteria* (November 16, 1955). In *Official Catholic Teachings: Worship and Liturgy*, ed. James J. Megivern (Wilmington, NC: McGrath Publishing, 1978), 139.

[8] Martin Hellriegel, "Holy Week: Some Reflections and Pastoral Suggestions," *Orate Fratres* 24 (1949–1950): 217.

know about your family, but mine would hardly call 5:50 a.m. Mass family-friendly!)

This parish's celebration of the Easter Vigil also began at an early hour on Holy Saturday morning. "In most parishes the blessing of the fire commences as early as seven o'clock [a.m.], in some even earlier," he writes, adding with a note of disappointment at the low turnout at his parish, "I was not too edified when at my first Holy Saturday as pastor (1941), I saw some 40 children and people grouped together about the new fire."[9]

But Father Hellriegel wasn't the only one who saw that things were more than a bit awry in the way the Church was celebrating the Easter Mystery at the time: Pope Pius XII also recognized that the Church's sacramental time was at odds with man's natural time. But unlike Father Hellriegel, the Holy Father possessed the power to restore the liturgies of Holy Week and return their celebrations to their original places during the day. As a necessary component of this 1955 restoration, Pius XII's instruction called for the proper liturgical formation of priests and laity. Priests, the decree's accompanying instruction says, "especially those who have the care of souls, are [to be] well instructed, not only concerning the ritual celebration of the restored Order of Holy Week, but also concerning its *liturgical meaning and pastoral purpose.* Let them, therefore, see to it that *the faithful also are more suitably instructed* during Lent in the proper understanding of the restored Order of Holy Week, so that they may take part in this celebration with intelligence and devotion."[10]

---

[9] Ibid., 221–222.

[10] "Instruction for the Proper Celebration of the Restored Order of Holy Week," Sacred Congregation for Rites, February 1, 1957, https://www.catholicculture.org/culture/library/view.cfm?recnum=11136, emphasis added.

More than sixty years after Pope Pius XII's Holy Week reform, the third edition of the Roman Missal continues to call for substantial catechesis on the Easter liturgies: "Pastors should not fail to explain to the Christian faithful, as best they can, the meaning and order of the celebrations and to prepare them for active and fruitful participation."[11] But there's good reason for the Church to remain vigilant in ensuring that the faithful be well versed in the details of the Easter celebrations. Even the most expert of liturgists can attest that the liturgy generally—and the Triduum liturgies particularly—can be both challenging to celebrate well and difficult to understand clearly. Overcoming these two challenges—to understand and celebrate the Easter mysteries—are the twin goals of this book.

A *Devotional Journey into Easter* offers insights into both celebration and understanding. In so doing, this book is simply carrying on the work begun by Pius XII—to ensure that the faithful, priests and laity alike, are better prepared to enter into the Paschal Triduum with clear heads and pure hearts. In helping the faithful better access the Easter Mystery, this book deliberately takes as its sources the Church's own: the rites and texts from the Roman Missal, the readings of the Lectionary, and the texts—particularly the patristic texts—in the Office of Readings for Lent and Easter. The book also relies on some contemporary Church texts, such as the 1988 Circular Letter on the Preparation and Celebration of the Easter Feasts, *Paschalis Sollemnitatis*, to help enhance the reader's understanding of the Lenten and Easter liturgies.

---

[11] Roman Missal, introductory instructions to the Sacred Paschal Triduum, no. 2.

The mystagogical method of teaching the liturgy you will find in this book is also from the Church. Mystagogical catechesis begins with the liturgy's various signs and symbols and uncovers their rich spiritual reality. As the *Catechism of the Catholic Church* (CCC) describes it, such liturgical instruction "aims to initiate people into the mystery of Christ (It is 'mystagogy') by proceeding from the visible to the invisible, from the sign to the thing signified, from the 'sacraments' to the 'mysteries'" (1075). Thus, from Ash Wednesday through the Paschal Triduum to Pentecost, the Church's liturgy presents a treasure of inestimable value — Jesus Christ our Lord — in sacramental signs and symbols. For example, *A Devotional Journey into Easter* uncovers how ashes, palms, and candles reveal Christ. The book also shows why words such as "Remember that you are dust," "I give you a new commandment," and "Behold the wood of the Cross" lead us to encounter Jesus the Word and reverberate with His wisdom. The book also reveals how processions, kneeling, and anointing can shape both body and soul to reflect the humble yet glorified Son of God. And — lest we forget where we began — the book also serves as a guide through the Easter calendar, showing how natural time's seasons, days, and hours usher in eternity during these sacred moments.

Pope Francis has remarked that "it is not enough to change the liturgical books to improve the quality of the liturgy. To do this alone would be a deception. For life to be truly a praise pleasing to God, it is indeed necessary to change the heart."[12] The restored rites of Holy Week have been with us for some time.

---

[12] Address to Participants of the Plenary Assembly of the Congregation for Divine Worship and the Discipline of the Sacraments, February 14, 2019.

Now is the time to understand these rites more deeply, celebrate them more faithfully, and participate in them more authentically. The time spent in studying the liturgy — and thereby celebrating it more fruitfully — promises nothing less than an opportunity to contemplate and encounter the eternal, in way that even St. Augustine would approve.

1

How to Enter the Combat Stupendous: Ash Wednesday and Lent

He is the mediator—the bridge, if you
will—between heaven and earth.

—Pope St. Paul VI[13]

An essential element of any journey, devotional or otherwise, is the destination. If I don't know where I'm headed, I can't expect to map an enjoyable and efficient course. The Israelites of the Old Testament wandered for forty years in the desert, even though they knew their destination. But had they lacked even that knowledge, their forty years may have become four hundred. Our modern travels—summer vacations to new places, business trips out of town, or even the quick jaunt to the local grocery store—also require clarity of purpose. Getting from point A to point B is impossible if you don't even know what point B is—or where it's located.

---

[13] *Liturgy of the Hours* (New York: Catholic Book Publishing, 1975), Office of Readings for the Thirteenth Sunday in Ordinary Time, vol. III, 419.

The same is true of our spiritual journey though Lent. What is its purpose? Where is it leading us? What is our destination? If we know on Ash Wednesday where we are headed and what is to become of us at Easter's grand conclusion, only then can we begin our trek with confidence—and in the sure hope of the resurrection.

So where are we journeying in Lent this year and, more broadly, in life now and forever?

The Church, who is both Mother and Teacher, goes to great pains to tell us about our destination throughout the Lenten season. On Ash Wednesday, for example, she reminds us of our goal as her priests bless the ashes:

> O God, who are moved by acts of humility and respond with forgiveness to works of penance, lend your merciful ear to our prayers and in your kindness pour out the grace of your + blessing on your servants who are marked with these ashes, that, *as they follow the Lenten observances, they may be worthy to come with minds made pure to celebrate the Paschal Mystery of your Son.* (emphasis added)

Further, on the First Sunday of Lent, we hear the following during the Preface at Mass (that is, the text immediately preceding the *Sanctus* or "Holy, Holy, Holy"):

> By abstaining forty long days from earthly food, he consecrated through his fast the pattern of our Lenten observance and, by overturning all the snares of the ancient serpent, taught us to cast out the leaven of malice, so that, *celebrating worthily the Paschal Mystery, we might pass over at last to the eternal paschal feast.* (emphasis added)

Are you beginning to hear a common theme, that is, a single destination—the Paschal Mystery? If so, you will find a further X marking the spot when you arrive at Palm Sunday, the doorstep of Holy Week. Prior to blessing the Palms for the procession into the Church, the priest introduces the celebration in these words:

> Dear brothers and sisters, since the beginning of Lent until now we have prepared our hearts by penance and charitable works. *Today we gather together to herald with the whole Church the beginning of the celebration of our Lord's Paschal Mystery, that is to say, of his Passion and Resurrection.* (emphasis added)

If you identified the Paschal Mystery as Lent's destination, your Lenten journey into the Easter Mystery is off to a great start. But let's consider what this Paschal Mystery is, and why it's the goal of Lent and of life.

The Church is adamant that all of her members come to an intimate knowledge of—and an actual participation in—the Paschal Mystery. After the rites of Holy Week and the Easter Vigil were restored by Pope Pius XII in 1955, there appeared much enthusiasm for the revised rites—at least initially. Since that time, in some places this eagerness to celebrate the Easter liturgies has waned. "Without any doubt," says the Church's instruction on the preparation and celebration of these feasts, "one of the principal reasons for this state of affairs is the inadequate formation given to the clergy and the faithful regarding the paschal mystery as the center of the liturgical year and of Christian life."[14]

The antidote to this inadequate formation, of course, is a greater familiarity with the Paschal Mystery, which is the

---

[14] Congregation for Divine Worship and the Discipline of the Sacraments, Circular Letter on the Preparation and Celebration of the Easter Feasts *Paschalis Sollemnitatis* (January 16, 1988), no. 4.

destination of our earthly devotional journey. For this reason, "catechesis on the paschal mystery and the sacraments should be given a special place in the Sunday homilies" during Lent.[15] But what's good for the flock is also good for the shepherd, the Church recognizes, and so, before paschal preaching is possible, priests in training "should be given a thorough and comprehensive liturgical formation" so that they "might live fully Christ's paschal mystery, and thus be able to teach those who will be committed to their care."[16] It can't be stressed enough how important this formation is for both priests and laity. Jesus' Paschal Mystery stands at the heart of His saving work and the center of the Easter Mystery. Lack of clarity on this central truth can result only in a wilderness wandering for the forty days of Lent. So, what *is* the Paschal Mystery?

The Paschal Mystery is "Christ's work of redemption accomplished principally by his Passion, death, Resurrection, and glorious Ascension," by which Jesus *passed* from the fallen world of sin to the heavenly world of the Father (see CCC 1067). These four distinct elements — suffering, death, Resurrection, and Ascension — are the substantial reality standing beneath each of Easter's sacramental signs and symbols. They are called "paschal" because they form, as it were, a bridge by which Jesus and those who belong to Him cross over — that is, pass over — to a new heaven and a new earth (see Rev. 21:1).

But let's take another step back and ask why Jesus needed to pass over from one side to another in the first place. Why did the chasm separating heaven and earth open? The answer to both

---

[15] Ibid., no. 12.

[16] Ibid., no. 43.

ASH WEDNESDAY AND LENT

questions is found "in the beginning," or at least nearer to it than we are now.

All created beings — earth, angels, man — find their source in the heart of the Trinity. When reading the first lines of the creation account, for example, we encounter these three Divine Persons: "In the beginning, when God created the heavens and the earth — and the earth was without form or shape, with darkness over the abyss and a mighty wind sweeping over the waters — Then God said: Let there be light, and there was light" (Gen. 1:1–3). God, who is Father, creates by His Word — "God said" — and is accompanied by the Spirit, the "mighty wind."

Creation, then, was from the start a reflection of the Trinity, who is a well-ordered family of loving Persons: God the Father utters His Son, the Word of creation, with the breath of the Holy Spirit. Pope Benedict XVI observes that "Creation is born of the *Logos* [that is, the Word] and indelibly bears the mark of the *creative Reason which orders and directs it*; with joy-filled certainty the psalms sing: 'By the word of the Lord the heavens were made, and all their host by the breath of his mouth' (Ps. 33:6); and again, 'he spoke, and it came to be; he commanded, and it stood forth' (Ps. 33:9)."[17] *Cosmos*, which in Greek means order and arrangement, is the root of the word *cosmetics*. Therefore, the cosmos was, from the start, *cosmetic*: a beautiful, well-ordered, living reflection of God.

But cosmos soon turned to chaos: ugliness, disorder, and death. Our state of original justice, giving to God what is due, was replace by original sin. As a concept, original sin is no easy truth for the intellect. In reality, though, original sin is as obvious as

---

[17] Pope Benedict XVI, Post-Synodal Apostolic Exhortation *Verbum Domini* (September 30, 2010), no. 8, emphasis in the original.

the sky is blue. English author G. K. Chesterton went so far as to remark that original sin "is the only part of Christian theology which can really be proved."[18] If you have any doubts, listen to a few minutes of any news broadcast—or just look around. But the universality of original sin aside, the nature of the Fall is difficult for man to understand. After all, why was eating an apple so wrong? And if Adam and Eve were already "like God"—they were made in His "image and likeness" (Gen. 1:26)—then why was falling for the serpent's temptation of being "like gods" (Gen. 3:5) so egregious? What's more, when God gave man a free will, wasn't the Lord just setting His creation up for the Fall? These are essential questions, for they have a direct bearing on the Incarnation of Jesus, and His eventual Paschal Mystery. To put it another way, the "Bad News" of the first Adam either enlightens or darkens the "Good News" of the second Adam, Jesus.[19]

Original sin is more than a matter of eating forbidden fruit —although that's an important detail to know. It's also more than our first parents merely wanting to be "like gods." Saints, after all, are called "saints" because they are *like God*. In fact, Lent, Triduum, and the Easter season work to make us more *like God* than our finite, myopic vision could ever understand: "Through the Spirit," says St. Basil the Great (d. 379), "we acquire a likeness to God; indeed, we attain what is beyond our most sublime aspirations—*we become God*."[20] Yet the forbidden fruit and the desire to be like gods back in the final days of Eden points to

---

[18] G. K. Chesterton, *Orthodoxy* (San Francisco: Ignatius Press, 1995), 19.

[19] "The doctrine of original sin is, so to speak, the 'reverse side' of the Good News" (CCC 389).

[20] St. Basil the Great, Office of Readings for Tuesday, Easter Week VII, vol. II, 976, emphasis added.

one unassailable truth of the Faith: our first parents' sin consisted in reaching for their eternal destiny — being like God — but "without God, before God, and not in accordance with God."[21] In other words, God had a plan from the beginning to lead His created order back to Himself in an unimaginable way (what the tradition calls the "economy of salvation"[22]). The Father's "two creating hands,"[23] the Son and the Spirit, would guide us to an even greater intimacy and "God-likeness" than "in the beginning." Our Fall — Adam's, Eve's, and ours today — results from our choice to get there our way, according to our own plan. But when this happens (as our experience confirms time and again), we jump the tracks, follow blind alleys, and find dead ends. Or, to put it simply, we reach the beginning of an abyss separating earth from heaven — and us from God. A bridge is needed so that we may *pass over* to the other side.

The period of the Old Covenant thus begins the initial stages of the greatest bridge-building project the world has ever seen. It was a work accomplished on a grand scale by Christ — the bridge that we cross on our way through the Easter Mystery. *Pontifex* means "bridge builder,"[24] and so Jesus is called. But He's not just any bridge builder, but the greatest builder of all times: He is the *Pontifex Maximus*.

The first great preparatory event for the Paschal Mystery, the bridge to heaven, occurs in Egypt. In fact, the entire Exodus account includes a series of events foreshadowing Christ's passing

---

[21] St. Maximus the Confessor, as quoted in CCC 398.

[22] See CCC 236.

[23] St. Irenaeus, in CCC 292.

[24] From the Latin, *pons*, "bridge," and *facere*, "to build."

over from life to death and from death to new life. For some four hundred years, the Chosen People, having once lived in honor, now reside in slavery. Hearing their cries and showing mercy on His people, whom He calls collectively His "firstborn son" (Exod. 4:22), God sends a series of plagues upon the land until, begrudgingly, Pharaoh sends the Chosen People away. In a sense, these plagues set the table for the Paschal Mystery. For, at the doorstep of their passage out of Egypt, the Israelites celebrate the first Passover ritual (an account read annually during the Liturgy of the Word at the Mass of the Lord's Supper). For this meal, a year-old, unblemished lamb is slaughtered. Its blood is painted around the doors of the Israelites' homes, and its flesh is eaten during the night, in the house, with unleavened bread. The Lord describes what will happen next:

> This is how you are to eat it: with your loins girt, sandals on your feet and your staff in hand, you shall eat like those who are in flight. It is the Passover of the LORD. For on this same night I will go through Egypt, striking down every firstborn of the land, both man and beast, and executing judgment on all the gods of Egypt—I, the LORD! But the blood will mark the houses where you are. Seeing the blood, I will *pass over* you; thus, when I strike the land of Egypt, no destructive blow will come upon you. (Exod. 12:11-13, emphasis added here and throughout this section)

That night, the Israelites left Egypt. After the Lord had passed over their homes, they would take a journey that led them to another kind of passover. With the Egyptians at their heels (since Pharaoh had changed his mind about releasing the Chosen People), and led by a pillar of cloud by day and a pillar of fire by night

(Exod. 13:21), God's children reach that great gulf between their old life in Egypt and a new life in the Promised Land—the Red Sea. But as the Israelites stand on the seashore, salvation history's first paschal bridge appears before them, with Moses at its head: "Tell the Israelites to go forward. And you, lift up your staff and, with hand outstretched over the sea, split the sea in two, that the Israelites may *pass through* it on dry land" (Exod. 14:15–16). This account from the book of Exodus, read each year at the Easter Vigil, anticipates what Jesus will do for us: lead us on a great crossing, a passage over a bridge from death to life, slavery to freedom, darkness to light.

The Exodus story presents perhaps the most prominent Old Testament account of the Paschal Mystery, but once the Jews experience this first Passover, the paschal motif starts appearing on a regular basis in salvation history. Consider the passage into the Promised Land after forty years of desert wandering. The Israelites are still east of the Promised Land in the territory called Moab, separated from their new home by the Jordan River. It sounds like a familiar predicament for God's people, and God's response is equally so. Recalling the great work He performed for His people in the Exodus account, "the LORD, your God, dried up the waters of the Jordan in front of you until you *crossed over*, just as the LORD, your God, had done at the Red Sea, drying it up in front of us until we *crossed over*" (Josh. 4:22–23). A later passover finds the great Old Testament heroines Naomi and Ruth journeying from Moab, a country afflicted with famine, to the rich harvest lands of Bethlehem in the springtime of the year (that is, during the time of the Passover ritual) in order to find abundant food and life in the bountiful fields of Boaz (see Ruth 1–2). Here again, the journey from suffering to abundant life involves the passage through a body of water, the Jordan River, which separates Moab from the Promised Land. The prophet Elijah also finds passage through water—building a bridge, like Moses, with the Lord's help. While journeying with his disciple, Elisha, Elijah was taken up into heaven by a fiery chariot only after he "took his mantle, rolled it up and struck the water [of the Jordan River]: it divided, and the two of them *crossed over* on dry ground" (2 Kings 2:8).

The above passages from death to life through water are preparations and prefigurements for history's greatest Passover, that of Jesus. Indeed, it is noteworthy that at Jesus' Transfiguration atop Mount Tabor, He appears with Moses and Elijah. These two Old Covenant bridge builders serve as significant witnesses to the work Jesus is about to undertake, the "exodus that he was going to accomplish in Jerusalem" (Luke 9:31): His Passion, Death, and Resurrection.

We see the first steps of Jesus' earthly passover in the Gospel of John. Here, while visiting the Temple during the feast of the Dedication, Jesus definitively proclaims that He is the Messiah. Answering the question about His identity, Jesus announces, "The Father and I are one" (John 10:30). The Jews, enraged at His answer, reply, "You, a man, are making yourself God." To this, Jesus replies, not without relevance to our current chapter, "Is it not written in your law, 'I said, *You are gods?*' " (John 10:33–34). Then Jesus "escaped from their power. He went back across the Jordan to the place where John first baptized, and there he remained" (John 10:39–40). After crossing to the east side of the Jordan, Jesus will then retrace the steps of the Israelites so that He, too, may cross back over the Jordan, in a renewal of that original entrance into the Promised Land. Reaching the heart of the Promised Land—that is, Jerusalem—He will suffer, die, rise, and ascend back to the Father. Like Moses and Elijah before Him, Jesus is building a bridge; but unlike the old bridges, which were mere shadows, Christ's bridge is the reality of the New Covenant. With His Resurrection, His bridge is built—and built to last.

In the texts examined so far in this chapter, we see how the Paschal Mystery stands at the center of salvation history. Original sin and personal sin cause chaos and separate us from God. Throughout the Old Testament, God prepares His people for the reunion of heaven and earth, so that we and all of creation can cross over from wilderness wandering into a land flowing with milk and honey. Jesus is history's Greatest Bridge Builder, the Pontifex Maximus, who, through His Paschal Mystery, definitively rejoins fallen earth to glorious heaven. The building and crossing of the paschal bridge is the goal of Lent, the purpose of the Triduum, the glory of Easter.

Now that we're properly oriented—provided with compass and map, as it were—let us go back to the beginning, to the dust from which Adam was formed, the dust we meet every year on an otherwise ordinary Wednesday in late winter. Let us consider how this Wednesday—Ash Wednesday—and the Lent that follows it offer us our first guidepost, directing our passover to Easter, a day on which all things will be made new.

Dust and ashes are distinguishing marks of Lent's opening days. It is no accident that the Ash Wednesday service is one of the most popular Lenten observances, even for non-Catholics. Even for the nominally religious, ashes on the forehead contain a certain symbolic appeal, speaking not only of our origins but of our end. For, as ashes are placed upon our heads, we hear the words, "Remember that you are dust, and to dust you shall return."[25] But Ash Wednesday is only the first step. As we go

---

[25] "Repent, and believe in the Gospel" is another formula given in the Roman Missal.

deeper into Lent, the liturgy further sharpens this focus on our ultimate destination. On the Sunday following Ash Wednesday, the First Reading presents the creation account, which takes us even further back to our dusty roots in the Garden of Eden.[26] Here we read how "the LORD God formed the man out of the dust of the ground and blew into his nostrils the breath of life, and the man became a living being" (Gen. 2:7). We were made from dust, and with the Fall we descend back into dust. We are reminded of this fact of life (and death) in the Ash Wednesday blessing over the ashes, when we "acknowledge we are but ashes and shall return to dust."[27]

But the ashes do more than recall our own fall: they should remind us that our transgression has turned the entire cosmos to chaos. We have brought down not just ourselves but all of creation with us. Not long after Adam and Eve's creation, "out of the ground the LORD God made grow every tree that was delightful to look at and good for food, with the tree of life in the middle of the garden" (Gen. 2:9). But with Adam's sin (the name *Adam* means "earth" or "ground"), all of the ground is cursed (Gen. 3:17), as well as the vegetation that comes from it. It is fitting, then, that Ash Wednesday's ashes are "made from the olive branches or branches of other trees that were

---

[26] Sunday readings occur on a three-year cycle (with the years designated by A, B, and C) and thus vary from year to year. Since the readings selected by the Church for the A cycle are especially sacramental and initiatory in character, however, these may be used each year, especially when a parish prepares candidates to receive the Sacraments of Initiation (baptism, confirmation, and the Eucharist) at the Easter Vigil. See *Paschalis Sollemnitatis*, no. 24.

[27] Roman Missal, blessing option 2.

blessed the previous year."[28] Earth's trees and plants that were once alive are themselves reduced to dust, as an anticipation of our own death.

So, Ash Wednesday and Lent, especially its early weeks, remind us (can we forget?) that we humans (*human*, like *Adam*, means "earthly") are given life from the ground by God's will, but that we shall return to the ground by the free choice of our will. Thus far, not a happy story. But at least there is nowhere to go but up!

But listen to the first words on the Church's Lenten lips. The entrance antiphon for Ash Wednesday declares, "You are merciful to all, O Lord, and despise nothing that you have made. You overlook people's sins, to bring them to repentance, and you spare them, for you are the Lord our God" (Wis. 11:24, 25, 26). True, we have reduced ourselves to dust, but this is not where the story ends (how sad for those who believe it is!). God's mercy, as Lent's first proclamation says, overlooks the chasm of our sins and restores us to life. As the psalmist puts it: "He raises the needy from the *dust*, lifts the poor from the *ash* heap, Seats them with princes, the princes of the people" (Ps. 113:7-8). If creation raised us from the dust, and original sin returned us to dust, Lent and Easter will raise us up once more and bring us across that bridge that separates us from God.

But passing over has never been an easy task. Moses found the work exhausting ("If this is the way you will deal with me," he complained to God, "then please do me the favor of killing me at once, so that I need no longer face my distress!" [Num. 11:15]). Joshua, who led the people into the promised land after Moses' death, also knew the difficulty involved in passing over.

---

[28] Roman Missal, rubric for Ash Wednesday.

Recall how he and Caleb encouraged the frightened people to enter the Promised Land: "If the LORD is pleased with us, he will bring us in to this land and give it to us, a land which flows with milk and honey. Only do not rebel against the LORD! You need not be afraid of the people of the land, for they are but food for us!" (Num. 14:8–9). Similarly, both Elijah and Ruth passed over to new life only by great effort and toil. Consider the anguished pleas of Elisha before Elijah, and Orpah and Ruth before Naomi, prior to their respective passovers (see 2 Kings 2; Ruth 1). Anyone who has ever prayed the Stations of the Cross knows, too, that the same exertions (and more!) accompanied Jesus' Passover (perhaps this is why both Moses and Elijah appear with Jesus at His Transfiguration — to give Him encouragement). The same challenge, too, opens before us in Lent.

Conclusion

The Church likens the Lenten season to climbing "the Holy mountain of Easter."[29] On the far side of the paschal bridge, from the vantage point of the Easter victory, the Church looks back on Christ's (and our) work and calls it a "stupendous combat," where death and life fought a bitter battle.[30] It's a battle worth fighting, and a battle we can win. But part of our success sees the goal, the end, the purpose: the Paschal Mystery, where

---

[29] *Paschalis Sollemnitatis*, no. 6.

[30] "Death and life have contended in that combat stupendous." From the Easter Sequence, *Victimae Paschali laudes*, sung before the Gospel acclamation on Easter Sunday and (as an option) throughout the Easter Octave. See *Lectionary for Mass* (New Jersey: Catholic Book Publishing, 1998), vol. I, 357.

we work with Jesus to span heaven and earth. And unless there is a bridge in our sights on Ash Wednesday, our journey through Lent risks ending where we began: right here in the fallen and dusty world of sin. It is a good thing we have a captain, coworkers, and tools necessary to win to victory. It's to these Lenten helps and supports that we will look in the next chapter.

In Brief

+ The reality of all things liturgical is the Paschal Mystery of Jesus: His suffering, death, Resurrection, and Ascension, by which He passed from the fallen world of sin to the heavenly world of the Father.

+ Through original sin, man disobeyed God's commands and chose, instead, to be like God *without* God, *before* God, and *not according to* His loving plan. In effect, original sin opened a giant chasm between earth and heaven, man and God.

+ God prepared to bridge heaven and earth in a variety of persons and events in the Old Covenant. Moses and the Chosen People passed over the Red Sea into the relative freedom of the desert. Joshua and God's Chosen People crossed over the Jordan River from desert death and wandered into a land of milk and honey. Elijah passed over the same waters of the Jordan before being taken up to heaven in a fiery chariot. Naomi and Ruth crossed over the Jordan once again from Moab's famine to Bethlehem's abundance.

+ Jesus builds history's definitive bridge by suffering, dying, rising, and ascending to the Father's right hand.

This saving Paschal Mystery is presented in a most powerful way during Lent and Easter so that Christ's Church and her members can join in the paschal work and pass over to heaven after Him.

✦ Ash Wednesday begins our bridge-building labors. In Lent's early days, the Church reminds of us of our origins from the dust, our eventual return into dust, and the Father's mercy, which reanimates us by the Spirit's power and the Son's saving work so that we may be citizens of heaven.

THE NEXT TIME YOU BEGIN LENT

✦ Know where you are going: to new life across Jesus' paschal bridge. Explain the Paschal Mystery to another person, such as a spouse, a child, a friend, or a parishioner.

✦ Since sin, original and personal, has gotten us into this fallen state, examine your conscience regularly, celebrate the sacrament of penance (that is, go to confession), and make concrete—even if small—resolutions to sanctity.

✦ Meditate upon the many Old Covenant figures who passed over before us. Listen carefully to the liturgy's prayers and readings, for they recall our sinful past and direct our present journey to heavenly glory.

2

How to Battle for the Paschal Mystery: Palm Sunday and Holy Week

Contend, O Lord, with my contenders; fight those who fight me.
—Entrance antiphon for Monday of Holy Week

Less than four months after the successful Allied D-Day landing on the beaches of Normandy, Operation Market Garden drove ground forces through occupied Netherlands and, with the help of British and American paratroopers, seized a number of bridges along the way—and ultimately battled for the Arnhem bridge over the Rhine into Germany. It was an ambitious plan, carried out bravely, with battles won and lives lost. But its goal, capturing the Rhine's bridge into Germany, was unsuccessful. It was, as one British general feared, "a bridge too far."

Lent's battle for the paschal bridge appears equally ambitious. We are in a life-and-death struggle—a "stupendous combat." Our victory lies on the other side of an arduous climb ("the Holy mountain of Easter"). We are bombarded at every moment with the deadly temptation to succumb, to wonder if we, too, are attempting

27

a bridge too far, with the Devil constantly standing in our way. Spanning the abyss of hell is dangerous work, and the stakes are never higher than during Lent's lead-up to Easter.

Yet we have a Captain leading our division against the opposing legions. Indeed, as we have seen in the previous chapter, He has done, and continues to do, the majority of the bridge-securing work. He knows what He is doing and where He is going with the perfect battle plan. As we will eventually pray after Easter during the Mass for the Ascension of the Lord, "where the Head has gone before in glory, the Body is called to follow in hope."[31] In addition to our Captain, a heavenly host of angels and an army of victorious saints accompany us, allied in our fight and flanking us on either side. We are also equipped by the Church with "weapons of self-restraint" (as the Opening Prayer for Ash Wednesday says), with fasting, with almsgiving, with prayer, and—perhaps most important—with the sacraments and sacramentals.

Ours is *not* a bridge too far—if we follow the plan laid out for us by the Church during Lent and, especially, during Holy Week. Christ and the members of His Mystical Body, aided by our self-discipline and sacramental weapons, will help us win through to the end. Let's look first at each of these combat-ready components of the liturgy generally and how they appear during Lent. We'll then consider how they perform as Palm Sunday inaugurates Holy Week.

Angels, Saints, and Sinners

Jesus truly is my personal Lord and Savior, but He fulfills this role in a corporate capacity, since He came to serve all and has

---

[31] Roman Missal, Collect for the Ascension for the Mass during the day.

made us each related to one another through Him. Each of us is an *individual* cell of a larger *corpus*, or body, the Mystical Body. The ancient Greek philosopher Aristotle recognized that man by nature is a social animal. Christian faith recognizes the same truth: individuals are born into a body and are saved as members of a body. Thus, we can rely on several communities to help us reach salvation—the hierarchy of angels, the Communion of Saints, and our own sacred society here on earth.

As for the first of these, the angels, as purely spiritual creatures, possess minds and wills and constantly behold the face of God, worshipping Him, honoring Him, and serving Him. They possess an extraordinary track record as God's commandos in the field. In the Old Covenant, for example, "they closed the earthly paradise; protected Lot; saved Hagar and her child; stayed Abraham's hand; communicated the law by their ministry; led the People of God; announced births and callings; and assisted the prophets" (CCC 332).[32] But their work continued into the New Testament as well, bringing great tidings to the shepherds and Mary and even poor, dumbfounded Zechariah, St. John the Baptist's father. Fortunately for us, they also show up for regular duty throughout Lent, in the same way they came to Christ's aid during His forty days in the desert. We hear in the Gospel for the First Sunday of Lent that after Jesus resists the Devil's three temptations, "angels came and ministered to him" (Matt. 4:11; Mark 1:13). At Lent's end, the Church recounts how an angel appears to strengthen Christ in His agony in the garden (see Luke 22:43).

---

[32] See Job 38:7 (where angels are called "sons of God"); Gen. 3:24; 19; 21:17; 22:11; Acts 7:53; Exod. 23:20–23; Judg. 13; 6:11–24; Isa. 6:6; 1 Kings 19:5.

Saints also accompany Jesus during His earthly journey to the Paschal Mystery, just as they support us during our liturgical celebration of the same mystery. His parents, for one, were particularly holy. For example, Mary, who, following the announcement by Gabriel (another angel!), offered her *fiat* and ushered in a new creation, is the pinnacle of human holiness. Likewise, the "just man" (see Matt. 1:19) Joseph was found worthy and thus chosen by God to wed Mary and to guard and protect the incarnate Son of God. We can't forget Jesus' cousin, John the Baptist, whom the Lord proclaimed to be "the greatest ever born of women" (see Matt. 11:11; Luke 7:28). The apostles, too, served as dependable aides-de-camp for Christ during His mission on earth. Despite their slow learning (see Matt. 13:36; Luke 24:25), human weakness, and alternate bouts of fear and rashness in the face of danger, these twelve men served as supreme confidants of Christ. As saints in the making, they should remind us of ourselves, and after Pentecost they should inspire us to be men and women with a passion for mission. Moses and Elijah, as we've already seen, also appear in cameos to "game-plan" with Jesus on Mount Tabor. Such a cast of supporting Gospel characters shows that holy people radiate God and thus show the way to heavenly brilliance.

But even those not yet perfectly holy — those of us struggling along the way — are a constant support to each other. In this world, the Church will always be a mixed bag of saints and sinners — but mostly sinners. Our mutual assistance should be a great comfort for us, just as it was for Jesus, as we travel with others in the Mystical Body. Indeed, liturgically speaking, we form a bond with our fellow pilgrims and, as the *Catechism* notes, "in the celebration of the sacraments it is thus the whole assembly that is *leitourgos*, each according to his function, but in the 'unity of the Spirit' who acts in all" (CCC 1144). Every man, woman, and child is enlisted as a unified army in retaking the paschal bridge. No one who is successful goes it alone.

Penance: Prayer, Fasting, and Almsgiving

Now let's look at some of the most effective weapons at our disposal during our Lenten battle. The Opening Prayer for Ash Wednesday makes clear the struggle opening before us, as well as the means to win through to the end. The priest prays: "Grant, O Lord, that we may begin with holy fasting this campaign of Christian service, so that, as we take up battle against spiritual evils, we may be armed with weapons of self-restraint."[33] Why will fasting and self-restraint serve us as sacred weapons as we push to the Paschal Mystery? Once again, we look to Jesus.

The Lenten liturgy recounts how Christ's saving work begins with fasting and prayer. On the First Sunday of Lent, we hear that "Jesus was led by the Spirit into the desert to be tempted by the devil. He fasted for forty days and forty nights, and afterwards he was hungry" (Matt. 4:1–2; Luke 4:1–2). Returning to Mass for Ash Wednesday, we hear the Church recall the prophet Joel's prescription to return to God "with fasting, and weeping, and mourning" in its First Reading (Joel 2:12), only to listen to Jesus elaborate on the penitential practices of prayer and fasting in the Gospel (Matt. 6:1–6, 16–18). Thus, as Jesus has done, so we do.

The Christian's three principal penitential practices, especially during Lent, are fasting, prayer, and almsgiving, "which express conversion in relation to oneself [i.e., fasting], to God

---

[33] Roman Missal, Collect for Ash Wednesday.

[prayer], and others [almsgiving]" (CCC 1434). But the Church offers *many* more ways of expressing interior penance, including:

> efforts at reconciliation with one's neighbor, tears of repentance, concern for the salvation of one's neighbor, the intercession of the saints, and the practice of charity, ... gestures of reconciliation, concern for the poor, the exercise and defense of justice and right (cf. Amos 5:24; Isa. 1:17), ... the admission of faults to one's brethren, fraternal correction, revision of life, examination of conscience, spiritual direction, acceptance of suffering, endurance of persecution for the sake of righteousness. (CCC 1434–1435)

The *Catechism* also includes the surest way of penance: "Taking up one's cross each day and following Jesus," as well as reading Scripture, and praying the Liturgy of the Hours and the Lord's Prayer (CCC 1435, 1437). These penitential acts and many more besides serve as effective means by which man defends himself and gains ground in the battle against Satan. It may be strange to think that we have the ability to go on the offensive against the Devil, but as our discussion that follows will show, penance allied to the sacraments serve as a one-two punch to the diabolical. There are, in other words, a multitude of penitential practices to punish the legion of demons who stand in the way of our taking heaven's gate.

Sacraments and Sacramentals

Curiously enough, the *Catechism* also includes the Eucharist as a means of penance, "for in it is made present the sacrifice of Christ which has reconciled us with God" (CCC 1436). Of course, the most obvious weapon at hand is the sacrament of penance, a particularly privileged means to encounter Christ and receive His forgiveness and saving grace. Both the sacrament of the Eucharist and the sacrament of penance throw the enemy into retreat mode.

Spiritual battle is largely a matter of ballistics training, for as Christians we have within our grasp those things we can hurl before the enemy to clear our path to holiness. *Ballistic* finds its origin in the Greek root *ballein*, which means "to hurl, toss, or throw," and it is a word that has landed in our Christian vocabulary in several ways. For instance, the Devil "is the one who 'throws himself across' God's plan and his work of salvation accomplished in Christ"—he is *dia-bolos* (CCC 2851). But we ought not to fear, because the Greek word also shows up in the term for exorcism in the New Testament: Christ Himself will "throw the Devil out"—*ex ballein*. And this same power to cast out the diabolical and win heaven shows up in a third example, the sacraments, which are a type of supernatural symbol that "throws together"—*sym-ballein*—heaven and earth in sensible signs.

With all these ballistics careening around in Scripture, however, it is most important to remember that the Paschal Christ, His Mystical Body of angels, saints, and sinners, and our own expressions of interior penance all exist today sacramentally. That is, each of these otherwise invisible and undetectable realities are "thrown together"—symbolized—in what can be seen, heard, felt, smelt, and tasted. That the sacraments come to us in such a human way, though, is no accident, for our present age, occurring after the descent of the Holy Spirit at Pentecost and before Christ's Second Coming, is called "the Age of the Church." In this age, the *Catechism* explains, "Christ now lives and acts in and with his Church, in a new way appropriate to this new age. He acts through the sacraments" (1076).

The first "sacrament" of His presence, however, is not one of the seven we find in our catechism; rather, it — quite literally — embodies all of them: the Mystical Body. Invoking a prayer used during the Easter Vigil, the Second Vatican Council reminds us that "it was from the side of Christ as He slept the sleep of death upon the cross that there came forth *'the wondrous sacrament of the whole Church.'*"[34] That is to say: as the first Adam lay sleeping in a garden and his side was opened and Eve, the mother of all the natural-born living, was taken forth, so now Jesus, the Second Adam, as he lies sleeping on a tree, has His side opened only to see emerge the Church, the mother of all of those born into a new supernatural life in Christ. For this reason, the Church is Jesus' "sacrament" in this age, His Body in Mystery, carrying on His saving work of throwing together heaven and earth in symbolic sacraments.

But, as we've noted, the Mystical Body as the main sacrament of Christ doesn't imply that we've thrown out the traditional seven sacraments. These, too, are filled with Jesus. Doctor of the Church St. Leo the Great (d. 461) tells us in a homily on Jesus' Ascension that "our Redeemer's visible presence has passed into the sacraments."[35] Another Doctor of the Church, St. Albert the Great (d. 1280), likened the Eucharist (and, by extension, the other sacraments) to the "the fruit of the tree of life" — that is, the Cross.[36] Like the Mystical Body, then, the sacraments join

---

[34] Second Vatican Council, Constitution on the Sacred Liturgy *Sacrosanctum Concilium* (December 4, 1963), no. 5.

[35] St. Leo the Great, Office of Readings for Friday, Easter Week VI, vol. II, 937.

[36] St. Albert the Great, Office of Readings for November 15 (St. Albert's feast day), vol. IV, 1560.

Jesus to us, giving us His very life and power, for our journey into the Easter Mystery. The same is true in a lesser way when it comes to the Church's sacramentals (e.g., blessed ashes, holy water, and palms) and her devotions (e.g., the Stations of the Cross). Even "sacramental things"—candles, words, church windows, feast days, bells, sacred music, vestments, liturgical colors—join us to Christ and His Church. Whether in the form of sacraments, sacramentals, or sacramental things, each of these symbols in its own way makes Christ's paschal action present today so that "the faithful are enabled to lay hold upon them and become filled with saving grace."[37]

As any Catholic well practiced in the liturgy knows, everything we've discussed so far—the saints, penitential practices, and sacraments—are present in the life of faith and its liturgical expression generally. But as our Lenten march through the desert draws to a close, we come to see how they truly come to life during the Holy Week liturgies, beginning with Palm Sunday.

Holy Week

When the Lenten season enters Holy Week on Palm Sunday, the battle for the bridge intensifies. Not only does Ash Wednesday's Collect emphasize our "campaign of Christian service" against spiritual evils and Easter's poetic Sequence recall life and death's stupendous battle, but so have the Fathers and saints of the Church. St. Ephrem (d. 373) speaks in graphic images about Christ's war against death and hell in order to lead us to heaven. He refers to Christ's incarnate body as "a chariot in which to ride

---

[37] *Sacrosanctum Concilium*, no. 102.

to the underworld," where He "invaded death's fortress, broke open its strong-room, and scattered all its treasure."[38] With Holy Week, the pitch of battle is upon us.

As Jesus' celebration of the New Passover was preceded by His triumphal entry into Jerusalem, so our liturgical celebration of these events begins with Palm Sunday. Here, at the beginning of Holy Week, we formally launch the final phase of our counteroffensive against the Devil as we are called upon to share in Christ's work in an especially intense way. Once again, as with Lent, Christ's squads of angels and saints and a custom-fit array of penitential weapons are at our disposal. But let us begin with a profile of our fearless leader — Jesus Christ — as He enters Jerusalem at the start of Holy Week on Palm Sunday.

Christ

Before any prayer is spoken, Palm Sunday's first rubric reminds us clearly: "On this day the Church recalls the entrance of Christ the Lord into Jerusalem to accomplish his Paschal Mystery."[39] Even the first words on the priest's lips during the Palm Sunday liturgy remind us of the paschal project for which we've been praying and fasting. Following the Sign of the Cross, he introduces the Mass in these words: "Dear brethren [brothers and sisters], since the beginning of Lent until now we have prepared our hearts by penance and charitable works. Today we gather together to

---

[38] St. Ephrem, Office of Readings for Friday, Easter Week III, vol. II, 735.

[39] Roman Missal, Palm Sunday, no. 1. See also *Paschalis Sollemnitatis*: "During Holy Week, the Church celebrates the mysteries of salvation accomplished by Christ in the last days of his life on earth, beginning with his messianic entrance into Jerusalem" (no. 27).

herald with the whole Church the beginning of the celebration of our Lord's Paschal Mystery, that is to say, of his Passion and Resurrection."[40] Even if we didn't know where we were going on Ash Wednesday, it ought to be clear to hearing ears on this day: with palm branches in our hands, we accompany Jesus into Jerusalem as He continues to complete His paschal bridge.

Our task, as with those who greeted Jesus with hosannas that day, is to follow Him closely and faithfully. Such, at least, is what the Church's liturgy tells us time and again. As the priest blesses the Sunday branches, for example, he asks God to "sanctify + these branches with [his] blessing, that we, who follow Christ the King in exultation, may reach the eternal Jerusalem through him."[41] Similarly, St. Athanasius (d. 373) teaches that "if we follow Christ closely we shall be allowed, even on this earth, to stand as it were on the threshold of the heavenly Jerusalem, and enjoy the contemplation of that everlasting feast."[42] Having entered the church after the Palm Sunday Procession, we hear the Opening Prayer summarizing these same sentiments: "Almighty, ever-living God, who as an example of humility for the human race to follow caused our Savior to take flesh and submit to the Cross, graciously grant that we may heed his lesson of patient suffering and so merit a share in his Resurrection."[43]

Each of Palm Sunday's liturgical rites — the blessing of palms and the reading of the Gospel account of His triumphal entry,

---

[40] Roman Missal, Palm Sunday, no. 5.

[41] Ibid., no. 6.

[42] St. Athanasius, Office of Readings for Sunday, Lent Week V, vol. II, 342.

[43] Roman Missal, Palm Sunday, no. 20.

the procession with palms into the church, as well as the solemn proclamation of the Passion—highlights the intense preparation for the Paschal Mystery, Christ's and ours.

Angels and Saints

We have seen how the angels and saints accompanied Christ during His earthly Passover and how they accompany us today. This heavenly host receives an honorable mention during Lent, and it is called upon to assist us now as it supported Christ during His Passover.

The Church suggests, for example, that the entrance "song" on Lent's first Sunday be the Litany of the Saints: "In the Mass of this Sunday, there should be some distinctive elements that underline this important moment (e.g., the entrance procession with litanies of the saints)."[44] In addition, throughout Lent's Sundays, the Roman Missal recommends the traditional "Stational Mass" with the diocesan bishop. At such Masses, ideally beginning at a location other than the main church where Mass will be celebrated, the bishop leads the whole body of the faithful in procession while "the Litany of the Saints is sung. Invocations to the Patron Saint or the Founder Saint and to the Saints of the local Church may be inserted."[45] In Holy Week, during the initiation of the elect (that is, those to be baptized), the Litany of the Saints is prayed once again. In each of these instances, we find the saints coming to our aid as angels and holy ones assisted Christ.

---

[44] *Paschalis Sollemnitatis*, no. 23.

[45] Roman Missal, rubric 1 prior to the beginning of Lent.

Perhaps our first inclination is to remember only those who oppose Christ in these darkest hours: Judas, Peter and the apostles, Pilate, Herod, the centurions, the scribes and Pharisees. But the Passion narratives read on Palm Sunday (and again on Good Friday), when heard carefully, reveal a great many who assist Christ: an angel strengthens Jesus in the Garden of Gethsemane (Luke 22:43), Simon of Cyrene helps carry His Cross (Matt. 27:32; Mark 15:21; Luke 23:26), women follow Him from Jerusalem up Calvary's hill (Luke 23:27), the centurion proclaims His innocence and divinity (Matt. 27:54; Mark 15:39; Luke 23:47), the good thief announces His power to save (Luke 23:40–42), the saints rise from their graves at His death and "enter the holy city" (Matt. 27:51–53), Joseph of Arimathea buries his body (Matt. 27:57–60; Mark 15:43; Luke 23:50–52), and Mary Magdalene looks on in sorrow and prayer (Matt. 27:61; Mark 15:47; Luke 23:55–56).

Angels and saints were strong companions during Christ's historical bridge building, and they are equally present and powerful to us today. Their presence is announced through the Lenten liturgy's Litanies of the Saints—who accompany a procession to the Heavenly Jerusalem—and proclamation of the Passion narratives.

Penance: Prayer, Fasting, and Almsgiving

We have heard already how the Church reminds us at the beginning of the Palm Sunday Mass that "since the beginning of Lent until now we have prepared our hearts by penance and charitable works."[46] If such has been the case, then Palm Sun-

---

[46] Roman Missal, Palm Sunday, no. 5.

day ought to find strong, ready, and willing hearts prepared for the paschal crossing. Throughout Lent, the Church says, "The faithful should try to attend weekday Mass and where this is not possible they should at least be encouraged to read the lessons, either with their family or in private."[47] Recall that the reading of Sacred Scripture is one of the many forms, and a particularly powerful form, of penance in the Christian life (see CCC 1437). The Sunday readings in particular are chosen to prepare us for the sacramental encounter with Christ during Holy Week and the Paschal Triduum. Throughout Cycle A,[48] for example, we hear of Jesus' fasting and temptations in the desert (Matt. 4:1–11), his Transfiguration (Matt. 17:1–8), the encounter with the Samaritan woman and her request for life-giving water (John 4:4–42), the restoration of sight to the man born blind (John 9), and the raising of Lazarus (John 11:1–44). Hearing the Passion (and Holy Week's other scriptural passages) in light of these Gospel passages will make the Word of God—"sharper than any two-edged sword" (Heb. 4:12), which is just what is needed during this week—into a powerful weapon. Praying with the Sacred Scripture "revives the spirit of conversion and repentance within us and contributes to the forgiveness of our sins" (CCC 1437), and so is an activity perfect for Holy Week.

---

[47] *Paschalis Sollemnitatis*, no. 13.

[48] The Sunday Gospels are arranged in a three-year cycle, A, B, and C. "The Gospel pericopes of the Samaritan woman, of the man blind from birth, and the resurrection of Lazarus are assigned to the III, IV, and V Sundays of Lent of year A. Of particular significance in relation to Christian initiation, they can also be read in years B and C, especially in places where there are catechumens." *Paschalis Sollemnitatis*, no. 24.

As noted above, prayer, fasting, and almsgiving constitute three privileged types of Lenten penance, but many more exist to aid the "campaign of Christian service." As the Lenten season intensifies during Holy Week, both Good Friday and Holy Saturday are best observed as days of fasting.[49] Almsgiving also intensifies during these final days of Lent, as Holy Week's Mass of the Lord's Supper includes the offerings of gifts for the poor, as well as bringing the Eucharist to those who are sick or homebound.[50]

Increased prayer also characterizes Holy Week's battle for heaven. St. John Chrysostom (d. 407) says of prayer that it is "the light of the spirit, true knowledge of God, *mediating between God and man*."[51] Mediating, of course, is the essence of Jesus' mission and of Holy Week: as Pontifex, He mediates and bridges earth and heaven so that we can pass over. For this reason, the Church states, "Devotional exercises that harmonize with the Lenten season are to be encouraged, for example, 'The Stations of the Cross'. They should help foster the liturgical spirit with which the faithful can prepare themselves for the celebration of Christ's paschal mystery."[52] Penance—whether prayer, fasting, almsgiving, or some other variety—paves the way to paschal victory during Holy Week.

---

[49] In addition to Lent's penitential fasting, Good Friday's and Holy Saturday's deprivations also indicate the Church's sorrow, for her "Spouse has been taken away." *Paschalis Sollemnitatis*, no. 39.

[50] Roman Missal, Thursday of the Lord's Supper, nos. 14, 33.

[51] St. John Chrysostom, Office of Readings for Friday after Ash Wednesday, vol. II, 69, emphasis added.

[52] *Paschalis Sollemnitatis*, no. 20.

Sacraments and Sacramentals

Lent is ordered from the outset to our participation in the Paschal Mystery of Christ, present in the sacraments. Catechumens prepare themselves through blessings, exorcisms, scrutinies ("rites for self-searching and repentance"),[53] and other minor liturgical rites prior to baptism, confirmation, and the first reception of the Eucharist at Easter. Those already initiated recall life's initial sacraments by Christian prayer and penance and by sacramental confession: the faithful "should approach the sacrament of penance during this season, so that with purified heart they may participate in the paschal mysteries."[54] The use of holy water, among the Church's many sacramentals, is an especially powerful aid as Lent terminates in Holy Week. Even though Lent can be likened to a desert, its journey is not to be waterless. On the contrary, since it can be desert-like (recall Jesus' time in the desert at the beginning of His public ministry), and since we are preparing to recount our baptism at the Easter Vigil in the form of the renewal of baptismal promises and the sprinkling with newly blessed water, the use of holy water is of great help.[55]

---

[53] "The scrutinies are meant to uncover, then heal all that is weak, defective, or sinful in the hearts of the elect; to bring out, then strengthen all that is upright, strong, and good. For the scrutinies are celebrated in order to deliver the elect from the power of sin and Satan, to protect them against temptation, and to give them strength in Christ, who is the way, the truth, and the life." *Rite of Christian Initiation of Adults*, no. 141.

[54] *Paschalis Sollemnitatis*, no. 15.

[55] In 2000, the Holy See responded to an inquiry about removing holy water from churches during Lent. "1) The liturgical legislation in force does not foresee this innovation, which in addition to being *praeter legem* [outside the law] is contrary to a balanced understanding of the season of Lent, which though truly being a season of penance, is also a

In addition to preparation for the sacraments and the use of sacramentals, the Holy Week liturgies are filled with some of the Church's richest sacramental sights. During this week, the diocesan bishop will bless the holy oils used in the celebrations of the sacraments: the Oil of Catechumens, the Oil of the Sick, and the Sacred Chrism. When consecrating the Sacred Chrism, for example, he will blow into the vessel, symbolizing the sending of the Holy Spirit. Holy Thursday will see humble foot washing; Good Friday, heart-felt kissing of the cross; the Easter Vigil, fire, candles, and smoke. In addition, as a pilgrim Church moving toward our Easter destination, a particularly rich and common sacramental experience during this week is processions.

Since bridge building is a process, the Church's liturgy sacramentalizes this truth by asking us to *process*—that is, to move in procession. Notice how many unique processions exist during Holy Week: Palm Sunday's procession into the church, Holy Thursday's procession with the Blessed Sacrament, Good Friday's procession-like movement to venerate the cross (it should be noted, in venerating the cross, we are not in true procession but move "as if in procession,"[56] since "the shepherd is struck and the sheep of the flock are scattered" [see Matt. 26:31; Mark 14:27], as the Marian Antiphon of Evening Prayer on Palm Sunday says),

---

season rich in the symbolism of water and baptism, constantly evoked in liturgical texts. 2) The encouragement of the Church that the faithful avail themselves frequently of her sacraments and sacramentals is to be understood to apply also to the season of Lent. The 'fast' and 'abstinence' which the faithful embrace in this season does not extend to abstaining from the sacraments or sacramentals of the Church." "Holy Water: Lent and Triduum," *Adoremus Bulletin*, December 31, 2007, https://adoremus.org/2007/12/31/holy-water-lent-and-triduum/.

[56] Roman Missal, Good Friday, no. 18.

and the Easter Vigil's procession from the dark night into the illumined church. Our spiritual Passover is sacramentalized in our very bones, on our two feet.

Prior to beginning the Palm Sunday procession, we hear how the "very large crowd spread their cloaks on the road, while others cut branches from the trees and strewed them on the road" (Matt. 21:8). We do the same in the liturgy, although our palms and praises now have a full, real, symbolic ("thrown together") meaning. St. Andrew of Crete (d. 740), in the Office of Readings for Palm Sunday, gives insightful instruction for our sacramental participation at this moment:

> Let us run to accompany him as he hastens toward his passion, and imitate those who met him then, not by covering his path with garments, olive branches or palms, but by doing all we can to prostrate ourselves before him by being humble and by trying to live as he would wish. Then we shall be able to receive the Word at his coming, and God, whom no limits can contain, will be within us.... So let us spread before his feet, not garments or soulless olive branches, which delight the eye for a few hours and then wither, but ourselves, clothed in his grace, or rather, clothed completely in him. We who have been baptized into Christ must ourselves be the garments that we spread before him.[57]

The liturgy—especially the Holy Week liturgies—offers a rich, sacramental tapestry of signs and symbols, each of which, in some fashion, make Jesus the Great Bridge Builder present

---

[57] St. Andrew of Crete, Office of Readings from Palm Sunday, vol. II, 419–420.

before us. Entering Holy Week with eyes and ears and senses attuned to the many ritual details, we perceive Jesus and His salvific work in great relief.

Conclusion

In a series of radio broadcasts during the Second World War, C. S. Lewis described our world as "enemy-occupied territory," and Christianity as "the story of how the rightful king has landed, you might say landed in disguise, and is calling us all to take part in a great campaign of sabotage."[58] He has landed indeed, infiltrating Satan's battle lines, and in His body—His "chariot," as St. Ephrem said—He is on a mission to conquer hell and reclaim man and all creation for His Father.

Holy Week makes Christ's saving mission present. Its liturgies are our chance to aid Him as His soldiers. Following Christ, accompanied by His angels and saints, fortified by penance, and armed with sacramental signs, we battle with Him unto His victory, and ours.

"Our pilgrimage on earth," St. Augustine says, "cannot be exempt from trial. We progress by means of trial. No one knows himself except through trial, or receives a crown except after victory, or strives except against an enemy or temptations."[59] Christ's enemy is engaged during Holy Week, and the battle against him is won at the zenith of the Paschal Triduum's bridge.

---

[58] These broadcasts formed the basis of what he would later publish in his 1952 book, *Mere Christianity* (Westwood, NJ: Barbour, 1952). The quote here comes from page 40 of the text.

[59] St. Augustine, Office of Readings for Sunday, Lent Week I, vol. II, 87.

It is to Holy Thursday, when Christ institutes the Holy Eucharist, that we advance next.

In Brief

✦ Jesus Christ acted in history to save the world and glorify God by His Paschal Mystery. This same Paschal Mystery is made present to us today through the Church's liturgy, of which Jesus continues to be the principle actor, its Prime Minister.

✦ Angels, saints, and holy men and women accompanied Christ during His life and throughout His Paschal Mystery. As we are called to join His work today, we are likewise supported and guided by God's holy ones, even as we assist others in Holy Week's battle for heaven.

✦ Fasting, penance, almsgiving, and prayer form an arsenal in Lent and Holy Week's spiritual battle. Although these means are necessary for the Christian life both during Lent and outside of it, the Holy Week liturgies call us to exercise them to follow Christ in His paschal struggle.

✦ Sacraments and sacramentals "throw together" heaven and earth, God and man, into a single whole. By these, we are united more closely to Christ and His Mystical Body as we work and pray for holiness, especially during Holy Week.

THE NEXT TIME YOU
ENTER HOLY WEEK

✦ Keep your eyes fixed on Christ by erecting seasonal images (such as Christ's triumphal entry into Jerusalem), and keep your ears attuned to His voice by meditating upon the readings for Sunday Mass and, if possible, for daily Mass.

✦ Invoke your patron saint, your parish's patron, your community's, or your diocesan patrons as well as your guardian angel. This "cloud of witnesses" (Heb. 12:1) will assist us to come to new life.

✦ Take up a notch whatever Lenten resolutions you have made. Even if your Lent has thus far been lackluster, make the best of this best week of the year. Pray, fast, and give alms as if it's the last Holy Week you will ever witness.

✦ Frequent regularly the sacraments of Penance and the Eucharist. Surround yourself with the Mystical Body's sacramentals, such as palms, holy water, and holy oil (at the Chrism Mass). These God-given gifts bond us to Christ in His death and victory.

3

How to Obey Orders: Holy Thursday's *Mandatum*

✠

I give you a new commandment.

—John 13:34

I admit that as a child I was annually confused about Thursday of Holy Week, called *Maundy Thursday*. Is it Monday? Or is it Thursday? It wasn't until much later in life that I discovered the *maundy* in Maundy Thursday comes from Jesus' command — or, in Latin, *mandatum*, "mandate" — to love one another (John 13:34). Holy Thursday is the day of the mandate, the day to "do this." Just what "this" is, we will discover in the following two chapters.

The Mass of the Lord's Supper on Holy Thursday also begins the "Sacred Paschal Triduum," as the Roman Missal calls it. The more commonly used name, Easter Triduum, while not incorrect, is not as accurate as Paschal Triduum. Paschal, as we have discovered, is the word par excellence for describing Jesus' work. His suffering, death, Resurrection, and Ascension compose His Paschal Mystery, His saving work whereby He bridges heaven and earth so that He — and we along with Him — may pass over from a fallen world to a heavenly world. *Easter*, whose etymology and origin is difficult to find,[60] seems to focus too narrowly on the Resurrection, however essential it is.

On this holiest of Thursdays, the Church's liturgy once again works as a true school of Christian formation, teaching us what we are about to embark upon. The Paschal Triduum begins by announcing the Paschal Mystery at the entrance antiphon for the Mass of the Lord's Supper: "We should glory in the Cross of our Lord Jesus Christ, in whom is our salvation, life and resurrection, through whom we are saved and delivered" (see Gal. 6:14).[61] Thus, as we enter Holy Thursday, the liturgy already looks ahead to Good Friday—"glory in the Cross"[62]—and also to the Easter Vigil—"salvation, life and resurrection." The Triduum is a *paschal* one, unfolding in many stages, from the beginning of the Mass of the Lord's Supper, through Good Friday, shining in the night of Holy Saturday, and ending at sunset of Easter Sunday.

This brings up another point of perplexity: How is it that Thursday to Sunday counts as only three days by the Church's reckoning? *Triduum*, after all, means this very thing: three days. At first blush, it seems as if someone didn't do the math. But if one starts with Thursday evening, and then counts to Friday evening (one day), then Saturday evening (the second day), ending with Sunday evening, the math adds up (even for a liturgist!).[63]

---

[60] Some suggest that *Easter* (or variations of it) refers to a pagan goddess, while others find its meaning in the "east" from which comes the dawn of a new day.

[61] Roman Missal, Thursday of the Lord's Supper, no. 6.

[62] This same entrance antiphon is used on September 14, the feast of the Exaltation of the Holy Cross.

[63] How Lent finds itself within forty days is equally mystifying! Counting from Ash Wednesday and ending on Holy Saturday yields forty-six days. Thus, some explanations begin counting on the First Sunday of Lent

The Paschal Triduum, in fact, has a history of complex cal-
culations. One faction in the early Church (among them, St.
Polycarp of Smyrna, martyred in 155) was called the "Quartodecimans," or, roughly, the "Fourteeners." They proposed that
Christ's Resurrection ought to correspond to the full moon
appearing on 14 Nisan, the night of the Jewish observance of
Passover (Nisan is the name of the springtime month in the
Jewish calendar, roughly corresponding to today's late March to
early April). Another group (often identifying Pope Anicetus
as its head) maintained that since 14 Nisan may fall on any
day of the week, a springtime Sunday, the day of Jesus' Resurrection, ought to stand as the principle determining factor in
celebrating the Resurrection. A compromise between these
two sides was ratified by the Council of Nicaea in 325, and
it has served the Church well through the centuries, even to
the present day. The Resurrection of the Lord is celebrated
on the first Sunday (satisfying Pope Anicetus) after the first
full moon of the spring equinox (contenting Polycarp and the
Quartodecimans). Thus, Easter may fall as early as March 22
or as late as April 25.

The astronomical and chronological symbolism of this time
of year is remarkable. Consider, first, what the stars tell us.
Looking up into the springtime (March–April) sky, we see the
constellation Aries, the Ram, speaking "in advance and for all
time, of the Lamb of God, who takes away the sins of the world

---

("The first Sunday of Lent marks the beginning of the annual Lenten
observance," says *Paschalis Sollemnitatis*) and end with Holy Thursday,
for a total of forty days. Another accounting multiplies six weeks of Lent
by six days each — Sundays not included — and then adds the four days
from Ash Wednesday to Saturday before Lent's first Sunday to make forty.

(John 1:29)."[64] There is also a "lunatic"[65] reality to the Paschal Mystery: 14 Nisan's full moon begins to wane on the day of Christ's victory. The Paschal Mystery also makes itself plain as the light of day. For with the passing of the spring equinox, daylight surpasses night and darkness, just as Jesus, the "light of the world," overcomes our life's gloom. This resurrection theme is also grounded in the earthly—and earthy—activities of spring. For during the springtime in the northern hemisphere, life reemerges from dormancy. In the trinity of its principal heavenly bodies—the moon, the sun, and the earth—the natural world reveals supernatural realities through the increasing life and light of springtime, even as the death and darkness of winter decrease.

Is it any wonder, then, that God chose this time of year to liberate the Chosen People from Egypt (Exod. 12:2)? That during this time of year, Joshua led the Israelites into the Promised Land (Josh. 5:10)? That in this season, Naomi and Ruth passed over from Moab to Bethlehem (Ruth 1:22)? Even Abraham, it is thought, went to sacrifice his son Isaac atop Mount Moriah on this day, only to replace him with a lamb (ram).[66] March 25 (roughly our equivalent of 14 Nisan) is a day unlike any other day. September 7, February 21, or July 10 (to take but a few random examples) cannot sacramentalize the Paschal Mystery of Christ as do the dates surrounding March 25. How fitting, then, that Jesus was conceived on March 25—and would die in accordance with this date. The symmetry here is not accidental, of course,

---

[64] Joseph Ratzinger, *The Spirit of the Liturgy* (San Francisco: Ignatius Press, 2000), 100.

[65] *Luna*, from which the English word *lunatic* derives, names the moon.

[66] Ratzinger, *The Spirit of the Liturgy*, 100.

but speaks to the same theme of death-in-life and life-in-death that embodies the Paschal Mystery.

It is to this same mystery that we now know Lent is leading us. We know, too, how we must approach its heavenly bridge: following the Paschal Christ, accompanying the angels and saints, arming ourselves with prayer and penance, and utilizing our sacramental armory. We even know why we are here, on Passover eve, the night on which Christ dined with His apostles for the last time before His Passion. We are, in short, in great shape on Holy Thursday to take our first step across the paschal bridge.

The Mass of the Lord's Supper, which inaugurates the Paschal Triduum, celebrates three interrelated mysteries of faith: the institution of the Eucharist, the establishment of the priesthood, and the command—the mandate—of brotherly love.[67] The next chapter will meditate upon the birth of the Eucharist and the priesthood on this night; the present chapter will look at the mandate and how the Church's obedient response to the mandate is sacramentalized in Holy Thursday's rites.

In numerous ways, Holy Thursday celebrates the Body of Christ: in the Eucharist and in the Church. Both are the Body of Christ, and each is related intimately to the other. The Church is commonly referred to as the Mystical Body of Christ, and the Eucharist as the true, real, and substantial Body of Christ. In the early Christian centuries, however, these terms were reversed: the Church was often called the "True Body of Christ," and the

---

[67] For this reason, "after the proclamation of the Gospel, the Priest gives a homily in which light is shed on the principal mysteries that are commemorated in this Mass, namely, the institution of the Holy Eucharist and of the priestly Order, and the commandment of the Lord concerning fraternal charity." Roman Missal, Thursday of the Lord's Supper, no. 9; also *Paschalis Sollemnitatis*, nos. 44–45.

Eucharist bore the name "Mystical Body."[68] The present use of these terms was due in large part to a change in mentality, language, and emphasis on the substantial presence of Jesus in the Blessed Sacrament. But is one designation more correct than the other? Which came first in time? And which comes first in priority?

Pope John Paul II offers the Magisterium's position on the matter in his 2003 Holy Thursday encyclical *Ecclesia de Eucharistia*. The pontiff notes that "the Eucharist builds the Church and the Church makes the Eucharist."[69] Both mysteries—the Church as Body of Christ, and the Eucharist as Body of Christ—came into being simultaneously at the original Mass of the Lord's Supper some two thousand years ago. It is for this reason that the *Catechism of the Catholic Church* rightly notes, "The Church is born primarily of Christ's total self-giving for our salvation, anticipated in the institution of the Eucharist and fulfilled on the cross." Today, therefore, in the "Age of the Church," the *Catechism* continues, she "exists in local communities and is made real as a liturgical, above all a Eucharistic, assembly. She draws her life from the word and the Body of Christ and so herself becomes Christ's Body" (CCC 766, 752).

But this same sense of the Church's connection to the Eucharist was present in the writings of the Church Fathers as well. St. Augustine offers a vivid reflection on the Mystical Body at prayer, especially its prayer during Lent, and how its pleading

---

[68] See Joseph Ratzinger, *Church, Ecumenism, and Politics: New Essays in Ecclesiology* (New York: Crossroad, 1988), 7.

[69] Pope John Paul II, Encyclical Letter *Ecclesia de Eucharistia* (April 17, 2003), no. 26.

voice arises as a unified whole from each of the smaller members who compose it. Augustine says:

> *Hear, O God, my petition, listen to my prayer.* Who is speaking? An individual, it seems. See if it is an individual: *I cried to you from the ends of the earth while my heart was in anguish.* Now it is no longer one person; rather, it is one in the sense that Christ is one, and we are all his members. What single individual can cry from the ends of the earth? The one who cries from the ends of the earth is none other than the Son's inheritance.... This possession of Christ, this inheritance of Christ, this body of Christ, this one Church of Christ, this unity that we are, cries from the ends of the earth.... The speaker shows that he is present among all the nations of the earth in a condition, not of exalted glory but of severe trial.... The one who cries from the ends of the earth is in anguish, but is not left on his own.[70]

No, we are not left on our own: St. Augustine here expresses in similar words the *mandatum,* Jesus' command to us. The Gospel for the Mass of the Lord's Supper offers not (as we might expect) an account of His institution of the Eucharist, as important as that is, but that other great moment in the cenacle — the Lord's washing of the apostles' feet. Through this humble act, Christ calls these first priests, and all of us, to love, serve, pray for, and care for others. As disciples of Christ, in other words, we are asked not to leave others on their own. The Gospel passage begins, "Before the feast of Passover, Jesus knew that his hour had come to pass from this world to the Father. *He loved his own in the world*

---

[70] St. Augustine, Office of Readings for Sunday, Lent Week I, vol. II, 87.

and he loved them to the end" (John 13:1, emphasis added). And insofar as we wish to be like Christ—to be like God—we, too, are ordered to do likewise for our neighbor, as we hear in the Gospel's final words: "I have given you a model to follow, so that as I have done for you, you should also do" (John 13:15).

When the Lord washed the feet of His apostles, He intended it as a symbolic action for the humility and love we must have in our hearts. Nonetheless, it is fitting that our response to Christ's order finds expression and realization in three ritual actions unique to the Mass of the Lord's Supper: the washing of feet, the presentation of the gifts, and the distribution of Holy Communion.

Washing of Feet

The washing of feet on Holy Thursday has taken many forms throughout the centuries, whether in cathedrals, abbeys, or churches; carried out by bishops, abbots, or priests; upon subjects who were clerics, monks, or the poor. The gesture is not intended to be a staged, historical reenactment (even though it is based on a historical reality), but a sacramental expression of Christ's humble gesture of charity and service.[71] The current instruction for the washing of feet allows pastors to "select a small group of the faithful to represent the variety and the unity of each part of the people of God. Such small groups can be made up of men and women, and it is appropriate that they consist of people young and old, healthy and sick, clerics, consecrated

---

[71] See, for example, the "Commentary concerning the Decree *In Missa in Cena Domini*" by the Congregation for Divine Worship and the Discipline of the Sacraments, January 6, 2016.

men and women and laity."[72] The action is informed not only by the Gospel narrative, but also by the various antiphons sung during the washing, including Christ's mandate: "I give you a new commandment, that you love one another as I have loved you, says the Lord" (see John 13:34).[73] Together, words and actions make Jesus and His humble gesture present and active so that we can join Him and work with Him in constructing the bridge from earth's humble, human shore.

Humility is the key to successful participation during the action for all involved: the priest who washes, the people who look on, and those whose feet are washed. In the same way that St. Peter protested, "You will never wash my feet" (John 13:8), many a proud heart may find it preferable to do the washing rather than receive the gesture. Yet, we must recall that Lent began grounded in humility—and so it is fitting that at its conclusion we should also be washed in humility. For we each began Lent nearly forty days before with a cross of ashes smudged on our foreheads. Now, from head to toe, we end Lent in humility as we prepare for Christ's Passion, Death, and Resurrection, with a thorough washing of our feet at our journey's conclusion. It is from the ashes and dung that we are washed, lifted up by God into the "company of princes" (see Ps. 113:7-8), after the model of Christ: "He emptied himself, taking the form of a slave, coming in human likeness; and found human in appearance, he humbled himself, becoming obedient to the point of death, even death on a cross. Because of this, God greatly exalted him" (Phil. 2:7–9, read on Palm Sunday).

---

[72] Congregation for Divine Worship and the Discipline of the Sacraments, Decree *In Missa in Cena Domini* (January 6, 2016).

[73] Roman Missal, Thursday of the Lord's Supper, no. 12.

Preparation of the Gifts

After the washing of feet, a second sacramental response to Jesus' command unfolds during the preparation of the gifts. At every Mass, the gifts and the altar are prepared, and this may include the bringing forward of bread, wine, and money or gifts for the poor or the Church.[74] These tangible offerings are necessary and good in themselves. But with them are brought each person's heart, his entire life and being, through his prayers, works, joys, and sufferings. For the human heart is the one thing that God will not—cannot—take; yet He will gladly receive. Thus, there is a true, sacramental relationship between our hearts and our gifts.

At the Mass of the Lord's Supper, the presentation of the gifts takes on even greater import. The Church says explicitly in her rubrics for this Mass that "there may be a procession of the faithful in which gifts for the poor may be presented with the bread and wine."[75] In no other Mass in the Missal is such an instruction found, but only on this day, when the Church highlights what Jesus has commanded: to "do this," to "love one another." We are called upon to offer not only bread and wine, but gifts for the larger Mystical Body. If these are true expressions of our hearts' desires, our hearts beat more fervently with Jesus' heart.

To help our heartbeat keep tempo with Christ's, the Church adds another sacramental element to the preparation of the gifts: the hymn "*Ubi caritas*" to accompany the procession. "Where Charity and Love Prevail" (*Ubi caritas*) was composed sometime

---

[74] *General Instruction of the Roman Missal* (GIRM), no. 73.

[75] Roman Missal, Thursday of the Lord's Supper, no. 14.

during the first Christian millennium and for most of its life has been sung during the washing of feet. Today it suitably amplifies the giving of one's gifts — and one's heart — to Jesus in His larger Mystical Body. Its text is as follows:

Antiphon: Where true charity is dwelling, God is present there.

By the love of Christ we have been brought together:
let us find in Him our gladness and our pleasure;
may we love Him and revere Him, God the living,
and in love respect each other with sincere hearts.

Antiphon: Where true charity is dwelling, God is present there.

So when we as one are gathered all together,
let us strive to keep our minds free of division;
may there be an end to malice, strife, and quarrels,
and let Christ our God be dwelling here among us.

Antiphon: Where true charity is dwelling, God is present there.

May your face thus be our vision, bright in glory,
Christ our God, with all the blessed saints in heaven:
such delight is pure and faultless, joy unbounded,
which endures through countless ages world without end.
Amen.[76]

Another unique feature of the *Ubi caritas* at the Mass of the Lord's Supper is that it is one of the few chants recommended by the Roman Missal for use at a given Mass.[77] That is, in nearly

---

[76] Ibid.

[77] The "O *Redemptor*" (O Redeemer) at the Chrism Mass — also ideally celebrated on Holy Thursday — is another example of a particular text

all other Masses, multiple options or general guidelines direct the music for the preparation of the gifts; but here the rubrics encourage a particular chant to accompany the procession. This fact should emphasize that charity is the order of the day.

As a final word on the preparation of gifts at the Mass of the Lord's Supper, St. Peter Chrysologus (d. 450) explains how fasting can be a form of almsgiving and how such giving ends in receiving grace:

> When you fast, see the fasting of others. If you want God to know that you are hungry, know that another is hungry. If you hope for mercy, show mercy. If you look for kindness, show kindness. If you want to receive, give. If you ask for yourself what you deny to others, your asking is a mockery.... When you fast, if your mercy is thin your harvest will be thin; when you fast, what you pour out in mercy overflows into your barn. Therefore, do not lose by saving, but gather in by scattering. Give to the poor, and you give to yourself. You will not be allowed to keep what you have refused to give to others.[78]

As St. Peter notes, we respond to Christ's mandate to love one another on Holy Thursday—whether in our prayers, our fasting, or our almsgiving. In so doing, we engage the enemy with Christ in His battle over hell's abyss.

---

and music that the Church puts forward for the Offertory procession. There are, of course, proper chants for the Church's various Masses found in the Roman Gradual (*Graduale Romanum*).

[78] St. Peter Chrysologus, Office of Readings for Tuesday, Lent Week III, vol. II, 231–232.

Communion to the Homebound

A third sacramental response to Christ's Holy Thursday command comes from the altar. As mentioned above, our love of the Church—the Body of Christ—belongs also to the Eucharist—the Body of Christ. As we've seen, such love is uniquely expressed in the washing of the feet of others and in the offering of gifts to others. As a pinnacle of our love for Jesus in His Church and in His Eucharist, we now bring the Eucharist down from the altar to members of the Church who are absent.

At the end of the Eucharistic Prayer, when we celebrate today what Jesus instituted then, the Missal recommends that we bring Communion to those who are absent. "At an appropriate moment during Communion," it says, "the Priest entrusts the Eucharist from the table of the altar to Deacons or acolytes or other extraordinary ministers, so that afterwards it may be brought to the sick who are to receive Holy Communion at home."[79] Since the Eucharist is "born" on Holy Thursday evening (more on this in the next chapter), the Church charges the faithful to go to the extra effort of helping all members of the Body of Christ receive the Body of Christ. After all, when Christ through the liturgy says, "*accipite, manducate, bibite*"—take, eat, drink—He isn't proffering an invitation but issuing a command!

Our response upon receiving the Eucharist, as St. John Chrysostom insists, ought not only to redound to our own spiritual benefit but also to immediately inspire us to respond in charity to our neighbor. "You have tasted the Blood of the Lord, yet you do not recognize your brother," St. John Chrysostom writes. "You

---

[79] Roman Missal, Thursday of the Lord's Supper, no. 33; also *Paschalis Sollemnitatis*, no. 53.

dishonor this table when you do not judge worthy of sharing your food someone judged worthy to take part in this meal. . . . God freed you from all your sins and invited you here, but you have not become more merciful."[80] His stern words warning communicants to care for the poor are equally applicable to our necessary care for the *poor in health*, the sick and homebound. The love of Christ—which is the substance of the Eucharist—"impels us" (2 Cor. 5:14) to love one another. For this reason, there are few greater ways to respond to Christ's mandate to love than when we bring the Eucharist to the infirm on Holy Thursday.

Conclusion

The Paschal Triduum launches in earnest with the Mass of the Lord's Supper. Through a tapestry of sacred signs and symbols, the Church's liturgy presents to us fundamental truths of Jesus' saving Paschal Mystery. As a constituent part of His saving work, He leaves us His Body and Blood in the Eucharist, institutes a visible priesthood, and demonstrates how to serve other members of His Body in humble service. The washing of feet, the offering of gifts to the poor, and the bringing of Holy Communion to the homebound sacramentalize our response to His command, His mandate, to "do this."

The Opening Prayer, or Collect, for the Mass puts it succinctly:

O God, who have called us to participate
in this most sacred Supper,
in which your Only Begotten Son,
when about to hand himself over to death,

---

[80] Quoted in CCC 1397.

entrusted to the Church a sacrifice new for all eternity,
the banquet of his love,
grant, we pray,
that we may draw from so great a mystery,
the fullness of charity and of life.

The "fullness of charity and life" are ours if we understand clearly and participate faithfully in these three elements of the Mass of the Lord's Supper. But to establish this charity in our hearts, we must also understand the font of such charity. For this reason, it is important to appreciate two other significant events that take place during the Church's Holy Thursday Mass: the institution of the Eucharist and the hierarchical priesthood, the topics of our next chapter.

In Brief

✦ The Paschal Triduum extends over three days—from the Mass of the Lord's Supper on Holy Thursday evening to the evening of Easter Sunday—and manifests to a superlative degree the saving paschal work of Jesus: His suffering, death, and Resurrection.

✦ The date of Easter is assigned to the first Sunday after the first full moon after the spring equinox. Nature's sun, moon, earth, and stars, coupled with the Old Covenant's various Passover sacrifices, make March 25 (or dates close to it) especially suitable to recount and relive Christ's paschal sacrifice.

✦ Holy Thursday focuses our attention on Jesus as He comes to us in the Church, His Mystical Body, and in the Eucharist, His Sacramental Body.

✦ Christ calls us to serve Him in the members of His Church. The Mass of the Lord's Supper signifies this call in its washing of the feet, the offering of gifts for the poor, and the taking of the Eucharist to those who are absent.

THE NEXT TIME YOU PARTICIPATE IN THE MASS OF THE LORD'S SUPPER

✦ Recall the many natural meanings that surround Holy Thursday: the sun's increasing light and warmth, the moon's sickly waning out of visible existence, the earth's return to life, and the twinkling stars of the heavenly ram. All reveal Jesus' Paschal Mystery.

✦ Focus your attention on the Paschal Christ as He manifests Himself in the Church, in His people, and in His Eucharist.

✦ Respond to Christ's command to "do this" by serving others, as exemplified in the washing of the feet, the giving of alms, and the offering of spiritual support to others. What specific actions can you make during these three holy days — and beyond?

4

How to Do This: Holy Thursday's Eucharist and Priesthood

He is the true and eternal Priest, who insti-tuted the pattern of an everlasting sacrifice.

—Preface for the Mass of the Lord's Supper

The Paschal Triduum generates life and meaning for the rest of the liturgical calendar. It is, in a sense, the "mustard seed" of sacred time. Buried (like Christ) in human time around March 25, it sprouts into "the largest of plants" (Matt. 13:32) and emerges as the center around which the hands of the liturgical year's clock revolve. Indeed, these three days—Holy Thursday, Good Friday, and the Easter Vigil—are their own sacred season, standing between the end of Lent and the start of Easter.

As we saw in the last chapter, Holy Thursday's Mass of the Lord's Supper contains unique liturgical elements. The same is true of the entire paschal celebration, which expresses its unique importance and integrity through the Introductory Rites and the Concluding Rites of the three Triduum liturgies. Let us, then, begin at the end. Can you recall how the Mass of the Lord's Supper concludes? The final words spoken are the priest's Prayer after Communion and the faithful's "Amen." There is no dismissal ("Go forth, the Mass is ended"). Instead, the faithful process through the Church with the Blessed Sacrament. At the following day's celebration, the faithful also recognize something different. Do you remember how the Good Friday liturgy begins? Following the priest's and deacon's prostration before the altar, they move to their chairs. At this point, we might expect the priest to make the Sign of the Cross and issue the familiar invitation "Let us pray." Instead, he offers the opening prayer for the liturgy. These peculiar endings and beginnings bind Holy Thursday to Good Friday in a real way.[81] The two liturgical celebrations (which are part of the Triduum's three-day liturgical celebration) draw meaning from each other: each needs the other to complete the image of the Paschal Christ—and win the battle for the paschal bridge.

The liturgical integrity expressed by the Triduum liturgies manifests the paschal unity of Christ's saving work: His humble service is embodied in the Eucharist, and His Eucharist anticipates His Cross, and His Cross leads the way to the Resurrection. Each is necessary, for half or even two-thirds of a bridge is as good as no bridge at all! The paschal synthesis found in Christ and His liturgy also ought to be reflected in our lives. The Eucharist is our main source of strength to serve others (in the *mandatum*), but to

---

[81] Further, the Good Friday liturgy never quite finishes—there is no blessing and dismissal, but, rather, after the Prayer over the People, all "depart in silence" (Roman Missal, Good Friday, no. 32)—and, at least until the third edition of the Roman Missal, Saturday's Easter Vigil did not begin with the Sign of the Cross.

appreciate the Eucharist, we first have to see the Cross—since the Body and Blood of Christ flow, literally, from His Crucifixion on Mount Calvary.

Likewise, Holy Thursday flows naturally into Good Friday (or, better, *from* the open side of Christ on Good Friday back into Holy Thursday). As we've already seen, the celebration that takes place on the day before Christ died, the Mass of the Lord's Supper, is a reminder that the Church and her members must respond to Christ's command to "do this," to "love one another." As we're about to see, Holy Thursday has another purpose as well. At Mass on Thursday evening, the Church also remembers (*remember* is the key word here—don't forget it!) our Lord's institution of the Eucharist and, as a necessary corollary, the priesthood, which will administer the Eucharist.

Institution of the Eucharist

Each of the liturgy's sacraments and sacramentals, every one of its signs and symbol, reach back to Jesus as their ultimate meaning. But because these holy signals of God's grace are grounded in the senses, in earthly things—whether baptismal water or holy water, for instance—they also naturally extend into the soil of human culture and, in particular, into the culture and practices of the Old Covenant.

Think, for example, about how bread comes to be on the human plane. First, the farmer plants a seed in the soil. Second, the buried seed begins its gestation and grows to maturity. Then, at harvest time, the farmer cuts each head of wheat and hands it over to the miller to crush into fine flour. The miller sells the wheat to the baker, who mixes the wheat flour with ingredients, sees the dough rise, and bakes it into bread. Finally, as his customers eat the bread, it is crushed once again. The "history of bread" (and, similarly, of wine) tells a story of death and resurrection, of dying and rising. Bread's natural history makes it a perfect character in God's supernatural history, and it is introduced at the world's first Passover, the account of which we read at the Mass of the Lord's Supper (Exod. 12:1–8, 11–14).

The Gospel reading at the Mass of the Lord's Supper conveys Christ's command of brotherly love through the account of our Lord's washing the apostles' feet. This command is preceded, however, by the First Reading, the Responsorial Psalm, and Second Reading, each of which recalls the Eucharist. Since, as we've already noted above, the two commands are not unrelated, it is fitting that the same relationship between the Eucharist and the *mandatum* should find a place in the Liturgy of the Word. In the First Reading, from the book of Exodus, chapter 12, the Church recalls the institution of the Passover meal in Egypt, on the night of the Chosen People's departure out of the land. The account begins with the Lord's directive to Moses: "This month shall stand at the head of your calendar; you shall reckon it the first month of the year" (Exod. 12:2). "This month" was the month of Nisan (at that time called Abib), which has helped the Church reckon its celebration of Easter. A springtime month, Nisan was a time of new growth. After the farmer planted his barley and wheat the year before, these crops grew throughout autumn before falling dormant in the winter. In the month of Nisan, these same crops have come back to life and reach maturity. This "month of ripe grain"[82] would

---

[82] The NABRE footnote to Exodus 12:2 explains: "Abib, the month of 'ripe grain.' Cf. 13:4; 23:15; 34:18; Dt 16:1. It occurred near the vernal

find the Chosen People harvesting the winter-turned-springtime crop, beginning the same process — from farmer to miller, from miller to baker, and from baker to customer — and revealing death and resurrection in each stage along the way.

Spring was also the month when new lambs were born. The experienced farmer, not wishing his newborn livestock to enter the world in the midst of winter, would arrange for their birth in the springtime, when warm air, running streams of water, and fresh fields of grass were available in abundance. Each lamb's first "birthday" thus fell in the springtime of the year. For this reason, the Lord also invokes the lamb as a part of the Chosen People's Passover meal:

> On the tenth of this month every one of your families must procure for itself a lamb, one apiece for each household. If a family is too small for a whole lamb, it shall join the nearest household in procuring one and shall share in the lamb in proportion to the number of persons who partake of it. The lamb must be a year-old male and without blemish. You may take it from either the sheep or the goats. You shall keep it until the fourteenth day of this month [that is, the time of the full moon], and then, with the whole assembly of Israel present, it shall be slaughtered during the evening twilight. They shall take some of its blood and apply it to the two doorposts and the lintel of every house in which they partake of the lamb. That same night they shall eat its roasted flesh with unleavened bread and bitter herbs. (Exod. 12:3–8)

---

equinox, March–April. Later it was known by the Babylonian name of Nisan."

Unleavened bread and the flesh and blood of a lamb were both essential to the Passover meal—both as part of their evening fare and also to serve as a sign that, as God's Chosen People, they were to remain untouched by death. But in addition to *what* they were to eat, the Lord instructs Moses and the people *how* to eat it:

> With your loins girt, sandals on your feet and your staff in hand, you shall eat like those who are in flight. It is the Passover of the LORD. For on this same night I will go through Egypt, striking down every firstborn of the land, both man and beast, and executing judgment on all the gods of Egypt—I, the LORD! But the blood will mark the houses where you are. Seeing the blood, I will pass over you; thus, when I strike the land of Egypt, no destructive blow will come upon you. (Exod. 12:11–13)

The Passover meal here described finds fulfillment by Jesus in His own Passover meal, held with His apostles. Like the Chosen People, He blesses bread—as St. Paul describes in the second reading, 1 Corinthians 11:23–26 (the earliest recorded account of the Last Supper). He similarly gives thanks over the meal's cup of wine—as we sing in the responsorial psalm, "Our blessing-cup is a communion with the Blood of Christ" (see 1 Cor 10:16). The "blessing cup" was the third of four cups that came to be used by the Chosen People when celebrating the annual Passover feast, and it was drunk after the meal's thanksgiving was offered. Christ is also present as the Paschal Lamb who was slain, whose blood averts death and gives life to those who celebrate—although in a new and more powerful way. St. John Chrysostom explains, "In those days, when the destroying angel saw the blood on the doors he did not dare to enter, so much less will the devil approach now when he sees, not that figurative blood on the doors, but the true blood on the lips of believers, the doors of the temple of Christ."[83]

There's another essential link between Christ's Passover and that of the Chosen People, a link also present in the Passover that Christians share with our Lord: *remembrance*. (Did you forget?) When the Lord finishes attending to the details of the traditional Passover meal—bread, lamb, eaten in a hurry while in the house—He concludes with one further feature in that original meal: a mandate issued to the Israelites that they remember the significance of the Passover celebration. He says: "This day will be a day of *remembrance* for you, which your future generations will celebrate with pilgrimage to the LORD; you will celebrate it as a statute forever" (Exod. 12:14, emphasis added).

A word or two about the power and significance of memory in the Old Testament will help us understand how it applies at the Last Supper. "Remembrance" for the Chosen People was no mere recollection of things long since passed. On the contrary, to remember the divine works of God actually made those events present and active in the present. Later in the Passover story, for example, when the Lord wishes to destroy the people after the Golden Calf incident, Moses implores him to *"Remember your servants Abraham, Isaac, and Israel, and how you swore to them by your own self, saying, 'I will make your descendants as numerous as the stars in the sky; and all this land that I promised, I will give your descendants as their perpetual heritage'"* (Exod. 32:13). Moses was not reminding God of something He had forgotten—as if He had a case of divine amnesia! Rather, he was imploring Him to act upon that past promise in the present.

---

[83] St. John Chrysostom, Office of Readings from Good Friday, vol. II, 474.

It is no coincidence, then, that Jesus uses the same word at the last Supper: "Do this in *remembrance* of me" (1 Cor. 11:24–25). The Greek New Testament communicates the same power of this command to remember through the word *anamnesis*. Forming the heart of this word is *mnesis*, or memory, just as a *mnemonic* device helps the mind remember. (For example, should we forget the nuts and bolts of construction we need only recall, "Right to tighten, left to loosen.") Thus, when Jesus tells us to celebrate the Eucharist as an *anamnesis* of Him, His same sacramental sacrifice is really, truly, and actually made present before us. The Mass is not a Passion play, but a making present of Jesus' Body and Blood, as real as it was two thousand years ago in the Upper Room. But we don't bring Christ back on our own—another sort of *mnemonic* device helps us with that task: "The Holy Spirit," the *Catechism* says, "is the Church's living memory" (1099, 1341). Thus, when the Holy Spirit "awakens the memory of the Church" (CCC 1103), Jesus' paschal sacrifice becomes present today—now—at this very moment. The *Catechism* explains:

> His Paschal Mystery is a real event that occurred in our history, but it is unique: all other historical events happen once, and then they pass away, swallowed up in the past. The Paschal Mystery of Christ, by contrast, cannot remain only in the past, because by his death he destroyed death, and all that Christ is—all that he did and suffered for all men—participates in the divine eternity, and so transcends all times while being made present in them all. The event of the Cross and Resurrection *abides* and draws everything toward life. (1085)

At the Mass of the Lord's Supper, we continue to step beyond this fallen world into the next, even as God and His saints come to meet us in the sacraments, especially the Eucharist. The famed fourth-century bishop St. Gaudentius of Brescia (a friend of St. John Chrysostom and ordained by St. Ambrose) expressed the realism of Christ's Eucharistic presence in today's age: "Daily it is before our eyes as a representation of the passion of Christ. We hold it in our hands, we receive it in our mouths, and we accept it in our hearts."[84] His words recall beautifully the Church's response to Jesus' Holy Thursday command to "do this in memory of me."

Another faithful reply to Jesus' Body and Blood concludes the Mass of the Lord's Supper. As noted above, once the priest offers the Mass's Prayer after Communion, a procession forms in which the Blessed Sacrament is carried through the church building to another place apart from the main altar. This practice, too, finds a prefigurement in the desert wanderings of the Chosen People: as they continued their journey on their way to pass over into the Promised Land, they were accompanied all the while by manna from heaven. So now a new Chosen People, the Church, is wandering in the desert, moving ever closer to heaven's promised land—and fed along the way by the true Bread of Life. The Holy Thursday procession features as yet another meaningful sacramental action.

When arriving at the altar of repose, the faithful—the Blood of Christ still fresh on the doorposts of their lips—remain before Christ and adore Him. While they do, the Church recommends reading Christ's discourse at the Last Supper from the Gospel of John (chapters 13–17)[85]—that period following the washing of the feet and institution of the Eucharist, but before His departure

---

[84] St. Gaudentius of Brescia, Office or Readings for Thursday, Easter Week II, vol. II, 670.

[85] See *Paschalis Sollemnitatis*, no. 56.

to the Garden of Olives. This discourse, which includes his "high-priestly prayer" as recorded in the Gospel of John (chapter 17), highlights another important component of the Last Supper: the institution of the priesthood. Without the Eucharist, the command to brotherly love is nearly impossible; but without the priesthood, the Eucharist *is* impossible.

Institution of the Priesthood

The Last Supper is both the "birthday of the chalice," as some in the tradition have called it,[86] and the "birthday of the priest-hood." The Eucharist and the hierarchical priesthood are, in a sense, twin brothers. Each exists for the sake of the other, and neither can exist without the other. The Preface for the Mass of the Lord's Supper (the prayer that immediately precedes the Sanctus, or "Holy, Holy, Holy") calls to mind both treasures:

> For he is the true and eternal *Priest*, who instituted the pattern of an everlasting *sacrifice* and was the first to of-fer himself as the saving *Victim*, commanding us to *make this offering* as his memorial. As we *eat his flesh* that was sacrificed for us, we are made strong, and, as we *drink his Blood* that was poured out for us, we are washed clean.[87]

The link between the Eucharist and the priesthood is both natural and essential, and it existed long before Holy Thursday.

---

[86] See, for example, Jean Gaillard, *Holy Week and Easter: A Liturgical Commentary* (Collegeville, MN: Liturgical Press, 1954), 60. Avitus of Vienne (d. 518) and Eligius of Noyon (d. ca. 650) also use the term; see the entry "natal day" in *The Catholic Encyclopedia* (1917), vol. 10, 709.

[87] Roman Missal, Thursday of the Lord's Supper, no. 16, emphasis added.

Etymologically, *panis* (the Latin word for "bread") and *pastor* share the same root, *pa*, meaning to feed, nourish, guard, or protect.[88] We've seen above, when considering the Eucharistic procession at the end of Mass, how Moses the mediator carried out his work with manna from heaven. Before him, the high priest Melchizedek offered bread and wine. Jesus, our "true and eternal Priest" (as the Preface for Mass calls Him) likewise gives bread as a part of His mediatorial ministry: He feeds the multitude with loaves and fishes, gives a "bread of life" discourse, and after His Resurrection, He breaks bread with His disciples on the road to Emmaus. All of these instances are related in some way to the Eucharist, but His most beautiful priestly pasturing—the feeding with heaven's own bread—comes to the world on Holy Thursday.

When Jesus gives the apostles the command to "do this as an *anamnesis* of me," He does, as He must, make them priests at the same time, bestowing on them the priestly power to confect the sacrament in His name. In today's Age of the Church, the period between Pentecost and Parousia, Christ comes to us in a most powerful way through the sacraments. He bestows His priesthood and its priestly power through a *sacramental character*, a mark or seal given by the sacraments of baptism, confirmation, and holy orders. Here again, knowing the origin of a word, in this case, *character*, can point us to its true meaning. A *charac*, in fact, is a sharp stick, pointed stake, or engraving tool. We might imagine that in the celebration of baptism, the Holy Spirit—the "artisan of God's masterpieces" (CCC 1091)—descends with His divine engraving tool and chisels upon the sacrament's recipient

---

[88] Similarly, based on the same root, *pa*, a *pantry* is a room for the bread, a *companion* shares one's bread, and a *panini* is a bread roll.

the *characteristics* of Jesus, who is prophet, king, and especially priest. Thus, by this sacramental character, "the Christian shares in Christ's priesthood" (CCC 1121; also *Compendium to the Catechism of the Catholic Church, 227*).

The sacramental character conforms us "on the outside" to Jesus and His work as prophet, king, and priest, but it also enables us to carry out these three saving offices. "Through Baptism and Confirmation, the priestly people is *enabled* to celebrate the liturgy" (CCC 1119; also 1273, 1304; emphasis added). As for the ordained, "these servants are chosen and consecrated by the sacrament of Holy Orders, by which the Holy Spirit *enables* them to act in the person of Christ the head" (CCC 1142; also 1581; emphasis added). As for the priests of the Old Testament, they remained "powerless to bring about salvation, needing to repeat its sacrifices ceaselessly and being unable to achieve a definitive sanctification, which only the sacrifice of Christ would accomplish" (CCC 1540). Today's unbaptized are similarly powerless, which is why RCIA (Rite of Christian Initiation of Adults) candidates are often dismissed from Mass prior to the Universal Prayer (also called the General Intercessions), the first instance of the Mass's priestly mediation, for without baptism, these candidates are powerless and unable to act in such a priestly way. It is not until after their baptism at the Easter Vigil that "the newly baptized participate for the first time" in the Universal Prayer.[89]

Christ's priesthood — along with the power to use it — is bestowed on all the faithful. Yet not all members of the Church share this office in the same way.[90] Through the sacramental

---

[89] Roman Missal, Easter Vigil, no. 58.

[90] "Though they differ from one another in essence and not only in degree, the common priesthood of the faithful and the ministerial or hierarchical

character of baptism, the recipient becomes a member of the Body of Christ and is enabled to become Jesus' coworker (a *pontifex minimus*, a "little bridge builder"!). By the sacramental character of holy orders, on the other hand, the priest shares in the work of Christ the Head (*in persona Christi capitis*, as the expression is). In this way, every man ordained a priest of the Church is enabled to carry out Christ's command in an indispensably different way from that of the baptized: he has the power to "do this," to consecrate the bread and wine into the Body and Blood of Jesus, and thereby make Christ's sacrifice actually present. The Mass of the Lord's Supper marks the anniversary of Christian priesthood—of the baptized and of the ordained. Yet the ordained priesthood rightly receives special treatment during Holy Thursday. Since the Paschal Triduum presents the story of Christ, the "true and eternal Priest," one of its central figures is the ministerial priest, for priests have become "sacramental signs of Christ" (CCC 1087).

The ministerial priesthood is so important to the Triduum that its emphasis extends far beyond the Mass of the Lord's Supper. The Chrism Mass, ideally held also on Holy Thursday, but legitimately celebrated on another day during Holy Week, clearly emphasizes the priest's role in the life of faith. At the Chrism Mass, the diocesan bishop not only blesses the holy oils used in the administration of the sacraments and some sacramentals (the Oil of the Sick, the Oil of Catechumens, the Sacred Chrism), he also concelebrates with his brother priests,

---

priesthood are nonetheless interrelated: each of them in its own special way is a participation in the one priesthood of Christ." Second Vatican Council, Dogmatic Constitution on the Church *Lumen Gentium* (November 21, 1964), no. 10.

leads them to renew their priestly promises, and encourages the faithful to pray for them.

The priestly emphasis is evident from the outset of the Chrism Mass. The entrance antiphon for Mass says, "Jesus Christ has made us into a kingdom, priests for his God and Father. To him be glory and power for ever and ever. Amen" (Rev. 1:6).[91] Later in the Mass, the bishop invites his priests to renew their promises made at ordination in these pontifical words: "Beloved sons, on the anniversary of that day when Christ our Lord conferred his priesthood on his Apostles and on us, are you resolved to renew, in the presence of your Bishop and God's holy people, the promises you once made?"[92] In particular, the Preface for the Chrism Mass announces the glorious role of the priest in the life of the Church:

> [B]y the anointing of the Holy Spirit you made your Only Begotten Son High Priest of the new and eternal covenant, and by your wondrous design were pleased to decree that his one Priesthood should continue in the Church.
>
> For Christ not only adorns with a royal priesthood the people he has made his own, but with a brother's kindness he also chooses men to become sharers in his sacred ministry through the laying on of hands.
>
> They are to renew in his name the sacrifice of human redemption, to set before your children the paschal banquet, to lead your holy people in charity, to nourish them with the word and strengthen them with the Sacraments.

---

[91] Roman Missal, Chrism Mass, no. 6.

[92] Ibid., no. 9.

As they give up their lives for you and for the salvation
of their brothers and sisters, they strive to be conformed
to the image of Christ himself and offer you a constant
witness of faith and love.[93]

As the Preface indicates, the priest renews, leads, nourishes, and
strengthens us. As Christ did these things two thousand years
ago, so He continues to carry these out through His priests. In
fact, as the Preface also indicates, priests are truly conformed to
Christ—so much so that they "give up their lives for [God] and
for the salvation of their brothers and sisters." Even as they give
life to the Church, these men are priests unto death.

The Renewal of Priestly Promises at the Chrism Mass ends
with the bishop's exhortation to the people to "pray for your
Priests, that the Lord may pour out his gifts abundantly upon
them, and keep them faithful as ministers of Christ, the High
Priest, so that they may lead you to him, who is the source of
salvation."[94] Seen in this context, a man who chooses to serve
as priest arguably may be undertaking the most dangerous job
imaginable, for the priest dares to mediate between heaven and
earth. Consider any instance of animosity between two parties:
warring nations, opposing cultures, divorcing spouses, fighting
animals. What is that person made of who would step between
them and bring about reconciliation? Now imagine that you are
about to step across the abyss of hell and mediate between God
and man. This, too, is no enviable task!

The psalmist recounts how God, in speaking to the Chosen
People, "would have decreed their destruction, had not Moses,

---

[93] Ibid., no. 12.

[94] Ibid., no. 9.

his chosen one, withstood him in the breach to turn back his destroying anger" (Ps. 106:23). His priestly, mediating, and pontifical work was so demanding that he complained to God, "If this is the way you will deal with me, then please do me the favor of killing me at once, so that I need no longer face my distress!" (Num. 11:15). Later, once the Chosen People came to the Promised Land and built Jerusalem, God looked for yet another priest to arbitrate His differences with the Chosen People—but without success: "Thus I have searched among them for someone who would build a wall or stand in the breach before me to keep me from destroying the land; but I found no one" (Ezek. 22:30). Ash Wednesday also anticipates priestly mediation, when, during the distribution of ashes, the Church sings of priests stepping between God's altar and His people: "Let the priests, the ministers of the Lord, stand between the porch and the altar and weep and cry out: Spare, O Lord, spare your people; do not close the mouths of those who sing your praise, O Lord" (see Joel 2:17; Est. 4:17).[95] The Church's priests, like Christ and the Old Testament priests before them, stand in the breach, offering their lives to reunite us to God. The bishop at the Chrism Mass is right: we need to pray for priests!

The importance of the ministerial priesthood is sacramentalized in a variety of other ways throughout the Paschal Triduum. At the Mass of the Lord's Supper and at the Good Friday liturgy, "the priest gives the homily," a function that, on other days, a deacon can fulfill.[96] At the Mass of the Lord's Supper, the priest,

---

[95] Roman Missal, Ash Wednesday.

[96] Roman Missal, Thursday of the Lord's Supper, no. 9; Good Friday, no. 10; it is unclear whether this direction excludes the deacon from preaching on these days.

and he alone, washes feet.[97] The Good Friday liturgy, even though it is not a Mass, "may not, however, be celebrated in the absence of a Priest."[98] During the showing of the cross from the sanctuary,[99] the priest himself is assigned the task of singing, "Behold the wood of the Cross."[100] And at the Easter Vigil, it is "the Priest [who] solemnly intones the Alleluia three times, raising his voice by a step each time."[101] In each case, the ordained priest—an "icon" of Jesus (see CCC 1142)—takes on unique roles to express the priestly work of Jesus.

Conclusion

St. John Vianney (d. 1869) is recognized as the patron saint of priests, particularly parish priests, because of his model of self-less service to his people. In his writings, he explains the dignity, beauty, and necessity of the priesthood—a glory received not only from Christ but from the pastoral care the priest gives to God's people. "Without the Sacrament of Holy Orders," he explains, "we would not have the Lord. Who put him there in that tabernacle? The priest.... Who feeds your soul and gives it strength for its journey? The priest. Who will prepare it to

---

[97] Roman Missal, Thursday of the Lord's Supper, no. 11.

[98] Roman Missal, Good Friday, no. 4.

[99] Versus the second form, when the cross is carried from the entrance of the church through the aisle to the sanctuary. See Roman Missal, Good Friday, no. 16.

[100] "He is assisted in singing by the Deacon or, if need be, by the choir." Roman Missal, Good Friday, no. 15.

[101] Only "if necessary, the psalmist intones the Alleluia." Roman Missal, Easter Vigil, no. 34.

appear before God, bathing it one last time in the blood of Jesus Christ? The priest, always the priest."[102] The Eucharist and the priesthood go together like love and marriage. For this reason, the celebration of both Christ's Blessed Sacrament and His sacred *pontifices* anticipate Good Friday's loving marriage of Christ the High Priest to His Bride, the Church. Jesus' *mandatum*, the Eucharist, and the priesthood are meaningless if not bridged (our theme continues) to His open heart upon Good Friday's Cross — our next step toward victory in the battle for salvation's bridge.

In Brief

✦ The Lord's initial instructions regarding the Passover meal in Egypt — eaten during the spring, in the evening, with unleavened bread and a year-old male lamb, immediately before passing over and out of Egypt — are fulfilled completely in Christ during His institution of the Eucharist on Holy Thursday.

✦ When Jesus tells His apostles, "Do this as a remembrance of me," their future recollections will, by the power of the Holy Spirit, not merely recall an event long since passed but will make Christ's saving self actually present.

✦ Sacramental character conforms the recipient to the priesthood of Jesus and enables him or her to exercise Christ's priesthood in some way. Through the common

---

[102] As cited in the letter of Pope Benedict XVI proclaiming a "Year for Priests" on the 150th anniversary of the "Dies Natalis" of the Curé of Ars, June 16, 2009.

priesthood, the baptized join their sacrifices to those of the ordained priest and offer them with Jesus to the Father; through the ministerial priesthood, the ordained stand in the person of Christ, the Head of the Church, and possess the power to transform the Mass's gifts into the Body and Blood of Jesus.

✦ The liturgies of Holy Thursday, Good Friday, and the Easter Vigil sacramentalize the priest's importance by the words, music, and actions they assign him.

THE NEXT TIME YOU PARTICIPATE IN THE MASS OF THE LORD'S SUPPER

✦ Read and meditate beforehand on the readings from the Mass, particularly the Lord's instructions to the Chosen People prior to their departure from Egypt. Connect the dots between these details and Christ's fulfillment of them on Holy Thursday.

✦ Spend time before the Blessed Sacrament following the Mass of the Lord's Supper and, as the Church suggests, meditate upon Jesus' words at the Last Supper (John 13–17).

✦ Attend the Chrism Mass, which is held on Holy Thursday or another day during Holy Week, and pray for your priests, for they were born, as priests, along with the Eucharist, on Holy Thursday.

✦ Notice the unique place the ordained priest plays in the Triduum liturgies: he washes the feet, shows the cross, sings the Easter Vigil's Alleluia. Because he is an incarnation of Christ the Priest, the paschal liturgies demand much of him.

5

How to Intercede for the World: Good Friday's Cross

We give glory to you, Lord, who raised up your cross to span the jaws of death like a bridge by which souls might pass from the region of the dead to the land of the living.

—St. Ephrem[103]

Not all battles in life's larger conflict are equally important. Prudence dictates that we choose, and choose carefully, the hill we wish to die on—if we have a choice in the matter at all. But sometimes that choice is made for us, as in this battle for eternal life. Consequently, when a group of warriors takes a strategically significant point—a hill, a bridge, or a city—they are told to hold it at all costs as an essential objective for victory.

One such hill in the Easter Mystery is Calvary, the steep incline outside Jerusalem's walls that may have taken its name from the bald outcrop of rock at its pinnacle. Calvary's high ground rises to strategic importance during the Triduum, for it represents not only a tactical necessity in the war against Satan

---

[103] St. Ephrem, Office of Readings from Friday, Easter Week III, vol. II, 736.

but also serves as the capstone in our paschal bridge to the Heavenly City. It must be taken, held, and fought for—even to the death. It *is* a hill to die on.

Like most battles, Calvary's hill is charred, ugly, and deadly, a fact indicated by its original Hebrew name, Golgotha, "place of the skull" (Matt. 27:33; Mark 15:22; Luke 23:33; John 19:17). So foul a place, Calvary almost appears a place *not* worth fighting for. The long-suffering, just man, Job, prefigures Christ our Captain in this battle to hell and back via earth's awful hill. "As Job sat on a dunghill of worms," writes the fourth century's St. Zeno of Verona, "so all the evil of the world is really a dunghill which became the Lord's dwelling place, while men that abound in every sort of crime and base desire are really worms."[104] Such a harsh appraisal of human existence, of course, must be put in the greater context of Christ's ultimate victory over mankind's "crime and base desire" on Calvary.

The Good Friday liturgy provides such a context as it remembers (and makes present: *anamnesis!*) the pitched battle of Christ and our own "campaign of Christian service," as Ash Wednesday called it. "On this day, when 'Christ our passover was sacrificed,' the Church meditates on the passion of her Lord and Spouse, adores the cross, commemorates her origin from the side of Christ asleep on the cross, and intercedes for the salvation of the whole world."[105] Our present journey into the Easter Mystery thus pauses—but does not rest—to meditate on three vital moments in the Good Friday conflict: the Passion and Cross endured by Christ, the Church's new life emerging from Christ's

---

[104] St. Zeno of Verona, Office of Readings for Saturday of the Eighth Week in Ordinary Time, vol. III, 286.

[105] *Paschalis Sollemnitatis*, no. 58.

opened side, and the act of priestly mediation expressed in the Solemn Intercessions.

Passion and Cross

As we enter Good Friday's celebration, it is important to keep in mind that the Good Friday liturgy is not a Mass. This fact itself should seem odd to us, since on every other day of the year the Church remembers Christ's priestly sacrifice precisely by celebrating the Mass. On this day, though, the Bride of Christ recalls her Spouse's saving work in other sacramental ways. Attentive ears will hear harsh yet life-giving truths in the liturgy's opening prayer. After priest and deacon prostrate themselves for a period of silent prayer, they return to their chairs and the priest prays: "*Remember* your mercies, O Lord, and with your eternal protection sanctify your servants, for whom Christ your Son, by the shedding of his Blood, established the *Paschal Mystery*. Who lives and reigns for ever and ever. Amen."[106] Just as the Father has not forgotten His mercy, we march onward over the paschal bridge, reminded through the reading of His word that Christ's work on Calvary is necessary in the war against death and sin.

The readings for the Good Friday liturgy paint a vivid picture of Christ's Cross and death. Turning first to the Old Testament, we hear Isaiah describing the gory details of the death of the suffering servant. But first he calls us to open our eyes and witness the outcome of this ordeal: "*See*, my servant shall prosper, he shall be raised on high and greatly exalted" (Isa. 52:13, emphasis added). Here and elsewhere during this liturgy, the Church calls

---

[106] Roman Missal, Good Friday, first option for the prayer, no. 6.

us to see for ourselves, to behold, *Ecce!* In the Gospel, we hear Pilate say, "Behold, the man!" (John 19:5). During the adoration of the cross, the priest draws our attention by proclaiming, "Behold, the wood of the cross!"[107] And before administering Holy Communion with the Eucharist held in reserve but not confected on this day, the priest exclaims, "Behold the Lamb of God."[108] Christ upon the Cross is a spectacle to behold and meditate upon throughout the year, but above all on this day.

But as Isaiah continues his prophecy, he reminds us that Christ's actions are focused on our own predicament:

> Yet it was our infirmities that he bore, our sufferings that he endured, while we thought of him as stricken, as one smitten by God and afflicted. But he was pierced for our offenses, crushed for our sins; upon him was the chastisement that makes us whole, by his stripes we were healed....
>
> Though he was harshly treated, he submitted and opened not his mouth; like a lamb led to the slaughter or a sheep before the shearers, he was silent and opened not his mouth. Oppressed and condemned, he was taken away, and who would have thought any more of his destiny? When he was cut off from the land of the living, and smitten for the sin of his people, a grave was assigned him among the wicked and a burial place with evildoers, though he had done no wrong nor spoken any falsehood. But the LORD was pleased to crush him in infirmity. (see Isa. 53:4–5, 7–10)

---

[107] Ibid., no. 15.

[108] Ibid., no. 26.

The Passion according to the Gospel of John for Good Friday (Palm Sunday uses accounts from Matthew, Mark, and Luke over its three-year cycle) completes and fulfills what was foreshadowed by Isaiah. The suffering servant of Isaiah is none other than Jesus. What was once only a shadow now suffers and dies in the flesh.

Pain, suffering, death, and destruction: Christ didn't win our redemption by these alone, although like any soldier who dies for his God, family, and country, our Lord wins great honor through such actions. Indeed, when a soldier's death is met with courage, bravery, and love of his country and comrades, his loss redounds to his merit. So, too, Christ: God the Father is not somehow pleased or satisfied because His only beloved Son is being tortured and murdered by us "worms," as St. Zeno suggests. Why, we should wonder, is not His anger inflamed all the more? No, on the contrary, since Jesus' heart was filled with humble love for, and obedience to, the Father, His sacrifice was accepted. The second reading for Good Friday, the Letter to the Hebrews, places obedience at the core of Christ's sacrifice: "Son though he was, he learned obedience from what he suffered; and when he was made perfect, he became the source of eternal salvation for all who obey him" (Heb. 5:8–9). Likewise, the verse before the Gospel (following the Lenten acclamation, such as "Glory and praise to you, Lord Jesus Christ!") contextualizes Jesus' suffering and sacrifice within the framework of humble obedience: "Christ became obedient to the point of death, even death on a cross. Because of this, God greatly exalted him and bestowed on him the name which is above every other name" (Phil. 2:8–9). Since it was Adam's disobedience that led the world in its fall, it is now the second Adam's obedience that raises it up.

But if the Church wants us to see what Isaiah, the Letter to the Hebrews, and St. John have seen, it does so with more than words. The Church's liturgy sacramentalizes humble obedience before our praying eyes and ears by turning the church interior into another corpse atop Calvary. After Holy Thursday's Mass of the Lord's Supper, the altar was stripped of its cloths,[109] not unlike Christ. In fact, prior to the Novus Ordo Missal following the Second Vatican Council, Psalm 22 accompanied the stripping of the altar on Holy Thursday:

> My God, my God, why have you abandoned me?
> Why so far from my call for help,
> from my cries of anguish?
> My God, I call by day, but you do not answer;
> by night, but I have no relief.
> They divide my garments among them;
> for my clothing they cast lots. (Ps. 22:2–3, 19)[110]

Thus, when the ministers enter on Good Friday, "the altar should be completely bare: without a cross, without candles and without cloths."[111] Here again, echoes of Job find voice in Christ, who is Himself the altar of His own sacrifice:[112] "Naked I came forth from my mother's womb, and naked shall I go back there" (Job 1:21). Christ the Head and His Body, the Church, are rendered stark naked and humbled as He enters the tomb. The priest and deacon

---

[109] Roman Missal, Thursday of the Lord's Supper, no. 41.

[110] The present Roman Missal also suggests Psalm 22 be sung during the distribution of Holy Communion on Good Friday (no. 28).

[111] Roman Missal, Good Friday, no. 3.

[112] "Because it is at the altar that the memorial of the Lord is celebrated and his Body and Blood given to the faithful, it came to pass that the Church's writers see in the altar a sign of Christ himself—hence the saying arose: 'The altar is Christ.'" *The Order of the Dedication of an Altar*, no. 4.

similarly lower themselves to the ground (the dust, we could say) to sacramentalize Jesus' humility and the Church's subsequent self-effacement.[113] "This act of prostration," the Church says, "which is proper to the rite of the day, should be strictly observed for it signifies both the abasement of 'earthly man' and also the grief and sorrow of the Church."[114] The mediating priest, recall, who debases himself as an incarnation of Jesus the High Priest — symbolizes the humility of Jesus, mankind, and the Church before the face of God.

But just as it seems we couldn't get any lower — just when the battle seems lost — a remarkable turn begins. For from Christ's humility (and ours) emerges His glory (and ours). From the ashes, dust, and dung of sin is formed a new creation. Pope Benedict XVI explains, "Indeed, Saint John's whole Passion narrative is built on this connection between humble service and glory (*doxa*): it is in Jesus' downward path, in his abasement even to the Cross, that God's glory is seen, that the Father and, in him, Jesus are glorified.... The hour of the Cross is the hour of the Father's true glory, the hour of Jesus' true glory."[115] Christ's Cross, planted in the depths of hell, also grows to the heights of heaven. Our return to the Father begins at this point. The Cross serves as the midpoint of the bridge, which through His death Christ has now crossed.

---

[113] Roman Missal, Good Friday, no. 5.

[114] *Paschalis Sollemnitatis*, no. 65.

[115] Pope Benedict XVI, *Jesus of Nazareth: Holy Week* (San Francisco: Ignatius Press, 2011), 75. The Holy Father spoke about the world's turn, now made present in the liturgy, in *The Spirit of the Liturgy*: "In liturgical celebration there is a kind of turning around of *exitus* to *reditus*, of departure to return, of God's descent to our ascent.... It is the turning point in the process of redemption. The Shepherd takes the lost sheep onto his shoulders and carries it home." Joseph Ratzinger, *The Spirit of the Liturgy* (San Francisco: Ignatius Press, 2000), 61.

For good reason, the Cross as the instrument of mankind's salvation has become the universal symbol of Christianity; and for good reason as well, the Cross is an integral part of the Good Friday liturgy. The Cross on which Christ suffered death is God's ultimate mechanism for raising up the fallen world, says St. Ignatius of Antioch (d. 108): "O what truly divine wisdom is this! O Cross, thou hoist to heaven!"[116] St. Ephrem, writing in his beautiful poetic style, also notes the Cross's instrumental role, saying that Christ "who was also the carpenter's glorious son set up his cross above death's all-consuming jaws, and led the human race into the dwelling place of life."[117] In the Cross, a work of man built from a work of nature, the artful language of theology and the organic expression of creation are both seeing the same thing.

Indeed, along with such artful analogies to the Cross, nature's simple yet powerful tree yields fruitful food for meditative thought. In the beginning, as the book of Genesis says, "the LORD God made grow every tree that was delightful to look at and good for food, with the tree of life in the middle of the garden and the tree of the knowledge of good and evil" (2:9). In the end, through Christ's victory, God promises mankind "the right to eat from the tree of life that is in the garden of God" (Rev. 2:7). At the center of salvation history stands the glorious, definitive tree of life. The Church's liturgy invokes ninth-century St. Theodore the Studite in the Office of Readings to help cultivate our appreciation of this tree:

> How precious the gift of the cross, how splendid to contemplate! In the cross there is no mingling of good and

---

[116] Quoted in Ratzinger, *The Spirit of the Liturgy*, 183.

[117] St. Ephrem, Office of Readings for Friday, Easter Week III, vol. II, 736.

evil, as in the tree of paradise: it is wholly beautiful to behold and good to taste. The fruit of this tree is not death but life, not darkness but light. This tree does not cast us out of paradise, but opens the way for our return.... This was the tree upon which the Lord, like a brave warrior wounded in his hands, feet and side, healed the wounds of sin that the evil serpent had inflicted on our nature. A tree once caused our death, but now a tree brings life. Once deceived by a tree, we have now repelled the cunning serpent by a tree. What an astonishing transformation![118]

Reflecting on St. Theodore's words, we would not be far from the truth to say that the history of salvation is really a history of trees. Christ's Cross—which is our tree of life—is precious; in fact, it is *adorable*. A significant feature of the Good Friday liturgy is therefore the adoration of the Holy Cross.

During this part of the liturgy, the Church offers a number of sacramental expressions that make clear the beauty of the Cross and its central place in our struggle toward heaven. The Good Friday liturgy, like any liturgy, is not a historical reenactment (such as we find in the medieval Passion plays), even though it is grounded in history. Rather, Christ's historical acts now abide in heaven and are, in some way, made truly present in the liturgy's sacramental signs.[119] For this reason, the very appearance of the

---

[118] St. Theodore the Studite, Office of Readings for Friday, Easter Week II, vol. II, 677.

[119] "Recalling thus the mysteries of redemption," teaches the Second Vatican Council, "the Church opens to the faithful the riches of her Lord's powers and merits, so that these are in some way made present for all time, and the faithful are enabled to lay hold upon them and become filled with saving grace." *Sacrosanctum Concilium*, no. 102.

cross during adoration is an important detail. Since Jesus' Cross was, as St. Theodore says above, "wholly beautiful to behold," Good Friday's cross should likewise be "of appropriate size and beauty."[120]

Other details abound throughout the adoration of the cross as well, including where and when the cross is revealed to the congregation. According to the rubrics, the priest may unveil the cross at the altar.[121] The altar, in addition to symbolizing Jesus, also represents His Cross. Relying on St. Epiphanius (d. 403) and St. Cyril of Alexandria (d. 444), the Church does "not hesitate to assert that Christ was the Victim, the Priest, and the Altar of his own Sacrifice. For in the Letter to the Hebrews, Christ is presented as the great High Priest who is also the living Altar of the heavenly Temple."[122] It is entirely fitting—and certainly not random—that the priest be asked to stand before the altar as he removes the violet veil from the cross in three stages, each time showing the cross and singing, "Behold the wood of the Cross, on which hung the salvation of the world. Come, let us adore."

---

[120] *Paschalis Sollemnitatis*, no. 68.

[121] The Roman Missal gives two options for the showing of the holy cross. In addition to the priest's showing of the cross in the sanctuary (described here), another option directs the deacon or priest to carry the unveiled cross through the nave of the church to the sanctuary, stopping at three points along the way and singing, "Behold the wood of the Cross ..." (see nos. 15–16). This latter form anticipates the entrance of the paschal candle into the Church at the beginning of the Easter Vigil, where the deacon stops at the same three locations and exclaims, "The Light of Christ."

[122] *The Order of the Dedication of an Altar*, no. 1.

During the adoration of the cross, the Roman Missal also directs that "only one Cross should be offered for adoration."[123] Singularity is a common sacramental device, meant to emphasize the one Redeemer. Church legislation and instructions, for example, desire only one altar, one tabernacle, one priest's chair, and (as we'll see) one paschal candle.[124] It might be argued that by making three crosses available for adoration, for instance, the pastor can remain faithful to the spirit of Good Friday by setting up a scene that resembles the crucified Christ with thieves on either side of Him (but does anyone wish to venerate the cross of the bad thief?). Yet the single cross focuses our attention on Christ alone. Recognizing the importance that the people place on adoring the cross on Good Friday, the Missal addresses concerns for time in a church full of the faithful: "If, because of the large number of people, it is not possible for all to approach individually, the Priest, after some of the clergy and faithful have adored, takes the Cross and, standing in the middle before the altar, invites the people in a few words to adore the Holy Cross and afterwards holds the Cross elevated higher for a brief time, for the faithful to adore it in silence."[125] But even in this alternative form of adoration, we can find precedent in salvation history. Our Lord Himself noted that we should once again look back to Moses and the pilgrim

---

[123] Roman Missal, Good Friday, no. 19. This instruction changes the former allowance that "In the United States, if pastoral reasons suggest that there be individual veneration even though the number of people is very large, a second or third cross may be used." Sacramentary, Good Friday, no. 19.

[124] See GIRM, no. 303 regarding the altar; Canon 938 §1 concerning the tabernacle; GIRM, no. 310 about the chair; and *Paschalis Sollemnitatis*, no. 82 on the paschal candle.

[125] Roman Missal, Good Friday, no. 19.

people for such a standard: "just as Moses lifted up the serpent in the desert, so must the Son of Man be lifted up, so that everyone who believes in him may have eternal life" (John 3:14–15, read during Mass on the Fourth Sunday of Lent, year B).[126] Individually or corporately, therefore, the cross is there to adore and remember as the high point of our Lord's Passion.

Moses' actions in the Old Testament give further insight into another instruction during the adoration of the cross. The Missal directs that "first the Priest Celebrant alone approaches, with the chasuble and his shoes removed, if appropriate."[127] In the book of Exodus, when God first called Moses, he did so through a burning bush that "was not being consumed" (Exod. 3:2). As he investigates this remarkable phenomenon further, God commands, "Do not come near! Remove your sandals from your feet, for the place where you stand is holy ground" (Exod. 3:5). The Good Friday wood — a tree on fire with God's love for man and our love for God in the person of Jesus — is similarly holy and approached with careful humility. Next, a new Chosen People follows the priest in adoring the cross in another sort of procession. After the priest, "the clergy, the lay ministers, and the faithful approach, moving *as if in procession*."[128] Another prophecy fulfilled, not only in history but in liturgy: "I will strike

---

[126] If the option of elevating the cross for all to venerate is chosen, rather than each one adoring during the liturgy itself, an "appropriate place (for example, the chapel of repose used for reservation of the Eucharist on Maundy Thursday) can be prepared within the church, and there the Lord's cross is placed so that the faithful may venerate and kiss it and spend some time in meditation." *Paschalis Sollemnitatis*, no. 71.

[127] Roman Missal, Good Friday, no. 18.

[128] Ibid., emphasis added.

the shepherd," the Passion according to St. Matthew says, "and the sheep of the flock will be dispersed" (26:31; also John 16:32).

Christ's Cross stands as the universal sacrament of salvation. Any and all who are saved come to God through the embrace of the Cross's arms, through the heart of the Eternal Word who hangs upon this everlasting tree of life. Universal salvation, in fact, is another principle theme of Good Friday, as the liturgy's extended Universal Prayer conveys. But before we consider these prayers, it is necessary to meditate upon the birth of the Church, the wedding of Jesus' Bride, and the new life this divine-human bond begets.

Birth of the Church and New Life

The Cross takes center stage on Good Friday not only as the key plank across the paschal bridge from earth to heaven, but also as the midwife for the Church. After all, the Church's sacramental birth, along with the birth of her sacraments, comes from Christ's open side upon the Cross. As noted in a previous chapter, the sacraments and the Church are integrally related: the Church being the great sacrament of Christ's redemption and the seven sacraments being particular streams of access to that same salvation. For this reason, there is a remarkable resemblance between the Church's seven sacraments and that other fundamental sacrament — the crucified Christ. Sacramental theology teaches that each of the seven sacraments combines words, or *form*, along with matter — that is, concrete things of the world. Baptism, for example, finds poured water (the matter) informed by the words, "I baptize you in the name of the Father, and of the Son, and of the Holy Spirit" (the form). Relying on Aristotle, St.

Thomas Aquinas (d. 1274) called such sacred matter-and-form composites *hylomorphic*: "wood" (*hyle-*) and "form" or "word" (*morphe*). Atop Calvary's hill, we see the source of sacramental hylomorphism: the Word of the Trinity upon the wood of the Cross. Word and wood together, Christ models and gives birth to every other sacrament, bringing together heaven and earth, God and man.

But the sacraments are nothing without the Church to administer them, of course. Therefore, intrinsically related to the blood and water pouring from Christ's side — symbols of the waters of baptism and the Blood of the Eucharist — is the birth of the Church herself. The sacraments are, in a sense, the Church's lifeblood, as St. John Chrysostom notes when he underscores the many ways in which the blood from Christ's side establishes the Church and her sacraments. First, he teaches that when "the soldier pierced the Lord's side, he breached the wall of the sacred temple."[129] God's Temple in Jerusalem served as one of many Old Testament figures of the Church (CCC 756). A place of daily sacrifice, its altar and inner court ran constantly with blood. This sacrificial blood flowed into subterranean streams flowing beneath the Temple within the rock of Mount Moriah. Together, the blood and water emptied into the Kidron Valley to the east or, depending on one's perspective, from the Temple's right-hand side. The opened side of Christ, the new Temple, which flows with blood and water, fulfills the opening from the old Temple and its flowing blood and water. Therefore, the Church is the visible temple of Christ, whose lifeblood is His Eucharistic Blood and baptismal water; and from the mourning songs of Good

---

[129] St. John Chrysostom, *Office of Readings from Good Friday*, vol. II, 474–475.

Friday, she will rise to sing of this glorious birth at the Easter Vigil during the sprinkling with the newly blessed baptismal water: "I saw water flowing from the Temple, from its right-hand side, alleluia; and all to whom this water came were saved and shall say: Alleluia, alleluia."[130] The new temple rises on Golgotha and reaches to heaven.

But let us look at another image of the nascent Church, this time as the New Eve vibrant with the nurturing life of the sacraments. Again, St. John Chrysostom leads the Church's meditations on this point for Good Friday. He says: "Since the symbols of baptism and the eucharist flowed from his side, it was from his side that Christ fashioned the Church, as he had fashioned Eve from the side of Adam.... As God then took a rib from Adam's side to fashion a woman, so Christ has given us blood and water from his side to fashion the Church. God took the rib when Adam was in a deep sleep, and in the same way Christ gave us the blood and water after his own death."[131] The Church thus becomes our mother; her womb, the baptismal font; her milk, the Eucharist. She gives new life, as we shall experience at the Easter Vigil.

New life indeed: the garden of paradise is restored to us. Following the Fall of our first parents, God "expelled the man, stationing the cherubim and the fiery revolving sword east of the garden of Eden, to guard the way to the tree of life" (Gen. 3:24). The blood of Christ, St. Leo the Great proclaims, opens the way to life once again: "The sacred blood of Christ has quenched the flaming sword that barred access to the tree of life. The age-old night of sin has given place to the true light. The Christian

---

[130] Roman Missal, Easter Vigil, no. 56.

[131] St. John Chrysostom, Office of Readings for Good Friday, vol. II, 474.

people are invited to share the riches of paradise. All who have been reborn have the way open before them to return to their native land, from which they had been exiled."[132] Like a film running in reverse, Christ undoes all that the first Adam had destroyed through his selfishness. The exile returns; the barren land springs again to life; sin is deleted from the accounting books; the security system keeping man out of Eden is disabled once and potentially for all. (But if you think Christ's blood extinguishing the cherubim's flaming swords is remarkable, wait until you see the script flipped altogether as Christ harrows hell!)

Good Friday has turned chaos back to cosmos, human isolation into trinitarian communion, death into life. St. Augustine could not have put it better, or more simply, when he explained the gift that Good Friday is to us: Jesus "effected a wonderful exchange with us, through mutual sharing: we gave him the power to die, he will give us the power to live."[133]

Universal Intercession

The Church demonstrates one further example of Christ's priestly sacrifice on Good Friday, an example that sacramentalizes again the truth and effects of Jesus' Paschal Mystery: the Solemn Intercessions. The reading from the prophet Isaiah that is used on Good Friday speaks of the suffering servant's justification of "many" and his taking "away the sins of many" (Isa. 53:11–12). Indeed, at the Last Supper, Jesus says that His blood "will be shed

---

[132] St. Leo the Great, Office of Readings for Thursday, Lent Week IV, vol. II, 313.

[133] St. Augustine, Office of Readings for Monday of Holy Week, vol. II, 432.

on behalf of many" (Matt. 26:28; also Mark 14:24). But who are these "many" we hear of on this day (as well as in Morning Prayer, or Lauds, on the Fridays of Lent)? The *Catechism*, relying on Scripture and Tradition, explains:

> He affirms that he came "to give his life as a ransom for many"; this last term is not restrictive, but contrasts the whole of humanity with the unique person of the redeemer who hands himself over to save us. The Church, following the apostles, teaches that Christ died for all men without exception: *"There is not, never has been, and never will be a single human being for whom Christ did not suffer."*[134] (605, emphasis added)

Thus, when we say that Christ reverses the damaging effects of sin once and potentially for all, we mean that, according to the Church, our Lord desires that all be saved, even if the fruits of His actions also depend on human free will to embrace those fruits. For Christ's blood does not wash over us and redeem us in some automatic, mechanical, or magical manner. Rather, His blood invites each to accept the free gift of salvation, as our first parents were free to accept or reject divine life with God. St. John Chrysostom explains: "Why of many, and not of all? Because not all believed. For He died indeed for all, that is His part: for that death was a counterbalance against the destruction of all men. But He did not bear the sins of all men, because they were not willing."[135] In other words, Jesus died for all, but His gift of new life must be received, not forced. For this reason,

---

[134] Council of Quiercy (853): DS 624; cf. 2 Cor. 5:15; 1 John 2:2.

[135] Homily XVII, Hebrews 9:24–26; see *Nicene and Post-Nicene Fathers*, ed. Philip Schaff (Peabody, MA: Hendrickson, 1994), 14:447.

the Church spends much of her Good Friday energy interceding for the whole world. Like Christ, she desires *all* to be included among the *many*.

Good Friday's Solemn Intercessions are remarkable for their length and completeness, especially when compared to the liturgy's more abbreviated version of these same prayers on all other Sundays of the liturgical year. And it is suitable that the Good Friday intercessions are so all-encompassing: since Jesus' Good Friday sacrifice is universal in scope, we intercede for the universe on this day. "The general intercessions are to follow the wording and form handed down by ancient tradition," the Church instructs, "maintaining the full range of intentions, so as to signify clearly the universal effect of the passion of Christ, who hung on the cross for the salvation of the whole world."[136] On this day, the Church, the fullest sacramental expression of Jesus' priesthood, intercedes for the Holy Church, the pope, all the faithful, catechumens, the unity of Christians, the Jewish people, those who do not believe in Christ, those who do not believe in God, those in public office, and those in tribulation.[137] Christ died for all, so the Church intercedes for all.

The manner of praying the Solemn Intercessions is similarly sacramental. Not only do the many categories of persons exemplify the universality of Jesus' sacrifice, but the many voices do as well. The deacon invites us to prayer, the people pray silently, the priest collects our individual prayers, and all voice an approving "Amen."[138] Even the priest's location during the Universal Prayer—standing,

[136] *Paschalis Sollemnitatis*, no. 67.

[137] Roman Missal, Good Friday, no. 13.

[138] Ibid., no. 11.

"if appropriate, at the altar"[139]—reveals a Good Friday truth. Christ the Priest mediates for the world from His altar, the Cross; likewise the ordained priest mediates for the world from the church's altar.

Conclusion

The Good Friday liturgy, like each of the sacramentally rich Triduum liturgies, offers many ways to join Jesus in His saving paschal work. Jesus certainly doesn't need our help in redeeming the world and glorifying His Father, but He wants it. He asks us to be His coworkers and soldiers in building and winning redemption's passage back to heaven.

As Holy Week and the Triduum approach, St. Gregory of Nazianzen (d. 390) outlines many manners of contributing to victory on Calvary's hill:

> We must sacrifice ourselves to God.... We must be ready to be crucified. If you are a Simon of Cyrene; take up your cross and follow Christ. If you are crucified beside him like one of the thieves, now, like the good thief, acknowledge your God.... If you are a Joseph of Arimathea, go to the one who ordered his crucifixion, and ask for Christ's body.... If you are a Nicodemus, like the man who worshiped God by night, bring spices and prepare Christ's body for burial. If you are one of the Marys, or Salome, or Joanna, weep in the early morning. Be the first to see the stone rolled back, and even the angels perhaps, and Jesus himself.[140]

---

[139] Ibid.

[140] St. Gregory of Nazianzen, Office of Readings for Saturday, Lent Week V, vol. II, 393.

If we actively share in Christ's battle to the death on Good Friday, we can look ahead to joining in His Resurrection at the Easter Vigil. As the apostle Paul encourages, "This saying is trustworthy: If we have died with him we shall also live with him; if we persevere we shall also reign with him" (2 Tim. 2:11–12). And after one more prayerful, reflective, silent day, a night unlike any other night will break upon us. But before the great Easter feast, there must be a final fast, and before the great Alleluia chorus, there must be a coda of utter and dismal silence on a day unlike any other day in the liturgical year: Holy Saturday.

In Brief

✦ Good Friday's climb to Calvary finds us in the heat of battle for our paschal return to God. The Cross stands at the Triduum's center of our passage: the Easter Vigil's new light shines upon Good Friday's Cross, casting its shadow onto Holy Thursday.

✦ The Good Friday liturgy celebrates three principal mysteries: the Passion and Cross of Christ; the birth of the Church, His Bride, from His opened side; and Christ's priestly mediation for the whole world.

✦ Christ's Passion and Cross are brought before us in the Liturgy of the Word — readings from Isaiah, Psalm 31, the Letter to the Hebrews, and the Passion according to St. John — and in our adoration of His Holy Cross. At the core of Jesus' sacrifice upon the Cross is His humble, obedient heart: because of this, the Father receives His sacrifice and exalts Him.

✦ The Church is born of blood and water flowing from Christ's side, much as blood and water flowed from the right side of Jerusalem's Temple. Similarly, as Eve was drawn from sleeping Adam, the Church, the New Eve, emerges from the New Adam asleep at the tree of the Cross. This new marriage begets new life in us.

✦ Since Christ died for all and offers salvation to all, the Church, His Body, intercedes for all on Good Friday.

THE NEXT TIME YOU ATTEND
THE GOOD FRIDAY LITURGY

✦ See in the cross you adore the wood of which our paschal bridge is built, the tree from which hangs Jesus, your soul's sustenance, and the sacraments that bring us face-to-face with God.

✦ Love your mother, the Church: her veins run with grace channeled from Christ's side, and she herself was born as the New Eve from the New Adam's rib. Like a natural mother, she gives life; but as supernatural mother, she bestows eternal life.

✦ Pray with clarity and intention for specific people in your life: a friend or family member who no longer believes; your bishop who leads you; the politicians who represent you; and all others. Be Christ's prayerful instrument and direct His channels of saving grace to particular persons in your life.

6

How to Go to Hell—and Come Back Alive: Holy Saturday's Silence

The bridegroom has been taken away.

—Tertullian, *De ieiunio* 2, 13[141]

Following Good Friday's pitched battle, Holy Saturday's silence finds our ears ringing. What to do today? Where are the liturgical rites to celebrate? Why do I seem to fumble and grope throughout the day? Each of the Triduum's days bears distinctive features. This Holy Saturday is unique in that it is nearly devoid of unique elements: minimal rituals, limited liturgies, few, if any, sacramental celebrations.

But there is much going on in the depths beneath this silent surface. Of all the reflections, thoughts, and writings of the past two thousand years about Holy Saturday, the Church has chosen an ancient and anonymous homily for the Office of Readings in the Liturgy of the Hours on this day. It is reprinted here in full

---

[141] As referenced in *Paschalis Sollemnitatis*, no. 39.

so that we might deepen our prayer on this extraordinary day, as Christ plumbs the depths of hell.

Something strange is happening—there is a great silence on earth today, a great silence and stillness. The whole earth keeps silence because the King is asleep. The earth trembled and is still because God has fallen asleep in the flesh and he has raised up all who have slept ever since the world began. God has died in the flesh and Hell trembles with fear. He has gone to search for our first parent, as for a lost sheep. Greatly desiring to visit those who live in darkness and in the shadow of death, he has gone to free from sorrow the captives Adam and Eve, he who is both God and the Son of Eve. The Lord approached them bearing the Cross, the weapon that had won him the victory. At the sight of him Adam, the first man he had created, struck his breast in terror and cried out to everyone, "My Lord be with you all." Christ answered him: "And with your spirit." He took him by the hand and raised him up, saying: "Awake, O sleeper, and rise from the dead, and Christ will give you light."

I am your God, who for your sake have become your son. Out of love for you and your descendants I now by my own authority command all who are held in bondage to come forth, all who are in darkness to be enlightened, all who are sleeping to arise. I order you, O sleeper, to awake. I did not create you to be held a prisoner in hell. Rise from the dead, for I am the life of the dead. Rise up, work of my hands, you who were created in my image. Rise, let us leave this place, for you are in me and I in you; together we form one person and cannot be separated.

For your sake I, your God, became your son; I, the Lord, took the form of a slave; I, whose home is above the heavens, descended to the earth and beneath the earth. For your sake, for the sake of man, I became like a man without help, free among the dead. For the sake of you, who left a garden, I was betrayed to the Jews in a garden, and I was crucified in a garden.

See on my face the spittle I received in order to restore to you the life I once breathed into you. See there the marks of the blows I received in order to refashion your warped nature in my image. On my back see the marks of the scourging I endured to remove the burden of sin that weighs upon your back. See my hands, nailed firmly to a tree, for you who once wickedly stretched out your hand to a tree.

I slept on the Cross and a sword pierced my side for you who slept in Paradise and brought forth Eve from your side. My side has healed the pain in yours. My sleep will rouse you from your sleep in hell. The sword that pierced me has sheathed the sword that was turned against you.

Rise, let us leave this place. The enemy led you out of the earthly Paradise. I will not restore you to that Paradise, but will enthrone you in heaven. I forbade you the tree that was only a symbol of life, but see, I who am life itself am now one with you. I appointed cherubim to guard you as slaves are guarded, but now I make them worship you as God. The throne formed by cherubim awaits you, its bearers swift and eager. The bridal chamber is adorned, the banquet is ready, the eternal dwelling places are prepared, the treasure houses of all good things lie open.

The kingdom of heaven has been prepared for you from all eternity.[142]

Apart from the Liturgy of the Hours, the Church's relative dearth of words on Holy Saturday speaks volumes about the death of her Spouse. The Roman Missal contains only three small rubrics, but no actual prayer texts, for "on Holy Saturday the Church waits at the Lord's tomb in prayer and fasting, meditating on his Passion and Death and on his Descent into Hell, and awaiting his Resurrection."[143] On this day, she refrains from Mass and all other sacraments, except for Penance and Anointing of the Sick.[144] Communion is given only as Viaticum.[145]

The Church recommends three holy practices in place of Mass and the sacraments, three means by which we respond to Christ's call to awake, rise, and "leave this place," as the Office of Readings recounts.

1. *Pray the Office of Readings:* "It is highly recommended," the Church's few instructions of the day say, "that on this day, the Office of Readings and Morning Prayer be celebrated with the participation of the people."[146] Brevity is the soul of wit, they say. The Church's brief words—outside of the Liturgy of the Hours, there are

---

[142] From an ancient homily on Holy Saturday (author unknown), Office of Readings for Holy Saturday, vol. II, 497–498.

[143] Roman Missal, Holy Saturday, no. 1.

[144] Roman Missal, Good Friday, no. 1.

[145] Roman Missal, Holy Saturday, no. 3; also *Paschalis Sollemnitatis*, no. 75.

[146] *Paschalis Sollemnitatis*, no. 73.

no others on this day—are the soul of our new life, and even Christ's last laugh at the Devil's expense.

2. *Read, pray, meditate:* Read the word of God, perform an act of devotion, or meditate upon the "image of Christ crucified or lying in the tomb or the descent into hell, which mystery Holy Saturday recalls, [or] also an image of the sorrowful Virgin Mary."[147] These meditations and images may be done individually, with a family, or in a group.

3. *Fast:* Abstaining from food and drink remains a Christian's formidable weapon in his "battle against spiritual evils," as we prayed on Ash Wednesday. Even though Church law binds Catholics between the ages of eighteen and fifty-nine to fast on Good Friday,[148] "it is also recommended that Holy Saturday be so observed, so that the Church, with uplifted and welcoming heart, be ready to celebrate the joys of the Sunday of the Resurrection."[149] The Church's joy, and ours, will be all the more amplified if, in lament for Jesus' descent into hell, we fast in anticipation of His return.

Conclusion

"I did not create you to be held a prisoner in hell," our Holy Saturday homilist hears. "Rise from the dead, for I am the life of

---

[147] Ibid., no. 74.

[148] *Code of Canon Law*, canon 1251.

[149] *Paschalis Sollemnitatis*, no. 39.

the dead. Rise up, work of my hands, you who were created in my image. Rise, let us leave this place, for you are in me and I in you; together we form one person and cannot be separated." Praying the Liturgy of the Hours, meditating on the sacred image of Christ or His Sorrowful Mother, and holding fast against the temptations of the flesh are three tools to break the bonds of hell with Christ and arrive soon upon heaven's shore. Easter joy is on the horizon but has not yet arrived. Night still remains.

In Brief

+ During the day of Holy Saturday, Jesus' body lies in the tomb, while His divine Person descends to the depths, preaching the gospel even to the dead (1 Pet. 4:6) and freeing the just from Satan's captivity.

+ The Church, Christ's spouse, meditates on His death, prays and fasts in mourning, but looks ahead in hope for His return.

THE NEXT TIME
HOLY SATURDAY ARRIVES

✦ Pray the Office of Readings and also Morning Prayer from the Liturgy of the Hours.

✦ Read the accounts of the Passion of Christ. Pray for any and all needs in your life in personal prayer, or pray a particular devotion, such as the Rosary or the Stations of the Cross. Meditate on an image of Christ in the tomb or of His Sorrowful Mother.

✦ Fast from unnecessary food and drink.

7

How to Enter the Promised Land: The Easter Vigil's *Lucernarium* and Liturgy of the Word

✠

Tell the people of Israel to go forward.

— Exodus 14:15, RSVCE

Do you remember the night you died? Maybe not — perhaps you were too young. Either way, your death, which is as unique as your life, followed a single pattern. In one way, it's the same old story; yet in another way, this old story is really a new story.

In fact, it is the story of your baptism, your *dies natalis* into the life of the Faith.

It begins in the depths of night, a night unlike any other night. Even though it had been still and silent during the preceding day, an ever-increasing rumbling and reverberating grew even as the sun set. Along with this sunset, a bright and brilliant moon — comforting in its light, yet somehow sickly in its hue — emerged, only to begin its wane back to black.

In the midst of this night, somebody grabbed you by the hand and led you (and there were most likely others supporting you) by a light rising in glory from the east. Its rays were cloaked, as they took the form of a radiant cloud. But the cloud seemed also to pour down rain, for water rose all about you. And even though your companions were still with you, a beast of sorts — Leviathan — dragged you down into an even colder, blacker darkness. And as you breathed your last breath and all that you knew or did or hoped or loved seemed things of the past, a Lamb, standing as though it had been slain (how strange!), seized you from the grasp of your grappling, and you slipped through death's deadly fingers (which explains why you were covered in oil before your descent), and you emerged victorious on dry ground once again.

The darkness from which you departed was now bright as day. The place where you once lived looked different, its colors standing out in greater relief than before. The life you once had seemed dead — as, indeed, it was — replaced by a life pulsating (almost buzzing) with a new heart and a new spirit.

If you don't recall this deadly — and lively — passage once made in baptism, don't fret (even though it *was* the most important moment of your life: "Your birth would have been no gain, had you not been redeemed," the Easter Vigil's *Exsultet* reminds us). Each year, at the Easter Vigil, the Church retells your magnificent story. Still, if this is the most important chapter in our lives, and if we have heard it retold over and over again at Easter, why don't we recognize it? A pallid moon? A sea monster? A slain yet living Lamb? And us daubed with oil and drowned in water — yet not drowned? Do we remember any of this? What accounts for the apparent discrepancies between memory and reality?

As we pass into the Easter Vigil in the Holy Night, one essential element helps us understand what's going on. Or, rather, five key components: our senses. The reality of Jesus' Paschal Mystery — His suffering, death, Resurrection, and Ascension — and of our sharing in His victorious work presents itself to our five senses by means of sacraments and sacramental signs. Specifically, your life-death-life story takes the form of fire, incense, candles, and processing at the Vigil's opening; poetry and music during the Easter Proclamation, or *Exsultet*; biblical texts and prayers during the Liturgy of the Word; and water, oil, white gowns, and bread and wine during the celebration of the Sacraments of Initiation. To appreciate this greatest story ever told, and our roles in it, we need to bring to the liturgy our sacramental senses. Recall that to sense the sacramental realities of the liturgy, we must understand the mystagogical nature of the liturgy, that is, the invisible made visible through our senses. St. Ambrose (d. 397) makes this same point to his newly initiated neophytes: "Do not then believe only what the eyes of your body tell you. What is not seen is here [at the Easter Vigil] more truly seen, for what is seen belongs to time but what is not seen belongs to eternity. What is not comprehended by the eyes but is seen by the mind and the soul is seen in a truer and deeper sense."[150] Seeing "sacramental things with the eyes of the heart,"[151] as he says, and hearing sacramental sounds with the "ears of [our] heart,"[152] as his famed student, St. Augustine, writes, open before us heaven itself, the goal of our journey. As with all the liturgical elements

---

[150] St. Ambrose, Office of Readings for Tuesday of the Fifteenth Week in Ordinary Time, vol. III, 492.

[151] See Edward Yarnold, S.J., *The Awe-Inspiring Rites of Initiation*, 2nd ed. (Collegeville, MN: Liturgical Press, 1994), 125–126.

[152] St. Augustine, Office of Readings for Monday of the Ninth Week in Ordinary Time, vol. III, 292.

of the Easter Mystery, the Vigil provides an array of objects and actions for our senses. We have only to understand them, to be alert to their "truer and deeper sense," to know we stand now at the threshold of salvation.

At that same threshold are three significant actions that begin the Easter Vigil: the blessing of fire, the preparation of the paschal candle, and the procession into the church building. We'll then listen with sacramental ears to the Easter Proclamation and to the Liturgy of the Word. These liturgical actions and words represent our first steps into the Promised Land. In the next chapter, we will turn our mystagogical attention to the celebration within the celebration: the initiation sacraments of baptism, confirmation, and the Eucharist.

The Threshold: Night, Fire, Candle, Procession, *Exsultet*

Night

Night and darkness are the first signs of the Easter Vigil. The Roman Missal entitles this liturgy, "The Easter Vigil *in the Holy Night*" and directs that "the entire celebration of the Easter Vigil must take place during the night, so that it begins after nightfall and ends before daybreak on the Sunday."[153] And if this rubric weren't clear enough, its instruction on the Paschal Solemnity emphasizes the point: "This rule is to be taken according to its strictest sense. Reprehensible are those abuses and practices that have crept into many places in violation of this ruling, whereby

---

[153] Roman Missal, Easter Vigil, no. 3.

the Easter Vigil is celebrated at the time of day that it is customary to celebrate anticipated Sunday Masses."[154] The Vigil is not
just another Saturday evening Mass: it is the first Mass of Easter, a
Mass that is celebrated not in the blue hues of the afternoon or the
golden-red air of fading twilight, but in the pitch black of absolute
night. The symbolism of the blessing of the fire and of the paschal
candle will depend on this same pitch blackness.

But why does the Church insist that the blackness of night
is so significant for the Easter Vigil?

The answer to this question is found in what we already have
learned: each of the Triduum liturgies employs particular times
of day to make its point: the Mass of the Lord's Supper began
"in the evening,"[155] the Good Friday liturgy started "about three
o'clock,"[156] and the Easter Vigil commences "during the night."
In other words, time is a creature, and like all of creation, it
becomes an earthly medium though which God bestows divine
life. So it is that in darkness we await the light, and in so doing,
we share in the tradition of the Vigil. We might recall from our
reading at Holy Thursday's Mass of the Lord's Supper how the
Chosen People, about to embark on their own Passover, were to
eat their saving supper during the night, while "on this same night
[the LORD] will go through Egypt, striking down every firstborn
in the land, human being and beast alike, and executing judgment on all the gods of Egypt" (Exod. 12:8, 12). Ever since that
night, "all Israelites must keep a vigil for the LORD throughout
their generations" (Exod. 12:42). Similarly, when history's true

---

[154] *Paschalis Sollemnitatis*, no. 78.

[155] Roman Missal, Thursday of the Lord's Supper, no. 1.

[156] Roman Missal, Good Friday, no. 4.

Passover arrives and Jesus passes over from death to life, it is at night that "the Church keeps vigil, waiting for the resurrection of the Lord."[157]

Fire

Night has its own significance: darkness, ignorance, death, fear —and the darker the night, the more intense these elements are communicated as realities at the Easter Vigil. But the darkness also serves as a context of sorts for another of the Vigil's first symbols: the new fire. Here, as well, we recognize that the darker the night, the greater the opportunity for God to reveal Himself and for us to encounter Him (dusk doesn't do it!) at this lighting of the first Easter fire. Presuming weather or other circumstances are such that the fire can take place outside the church (that is, outside the sacramental Promised Land), the Roman Missal calls for a "blazing fire,"[158] whose flames, the Church says, "should be such that they genuinely dispel the darkness and light up the night."[159] Anyone who has attended a bonfire or sat around a Wyoming campfire knows exactly what the Church means here! Christ is the new light, the *Fiat lux* ("Let there be light") of the new creation. His radiance ought to be seen, even felt. Sensible sacramental signs are the key. Every detail of that fire burns with meaning, including, for instance,

---

[157] *Paschalis Sollemnitatis*, no. 77.

[158] Roman Missal, Easter Vigil, no. 8. But where, "because of difficulties that may occur, a [blazing] fire is not lit, a fire is adapted to the circumstances." Roman Missal, Easter Vigil, no. 13.

[159] *Paschalis Sollemnitatis*, no. 82.

the way it is lit. While matches or a Zippo lighter will do in a pinch, of course, the tradition of the Easter fire asks that it be lit with flint.[160] This stone reminds the faithful that Christ was buried in a new tomb "hewn in the rock" with "a huge stone across the entrance" (Matt. 27:60; also Mark 15:46; Luke 23:53). This stone vault — itself housing the Christ, "the cornerstone" (Matt. 21:42; also Mark 12:10; Luke 20:17) — sparks new life and light as its cousin, the Easter Vigil flint, does at the Easter Vigil.

After the priest and the people have gathered around the fire, the priest greets them "on this most sacred night, in which our Lord Jesus Christ passed over from death to life."[161] The Paschal Mystery or passing-over theme has accompanied us along the Lenten journey into the Easter Mystery. Indeed, as a bridge from earth to heaven, it is truer to say that it has been our very path, the stones beneath our feet. After the priest's greeting and introduction, he blesses the fire in these words:

> O God, who through your Son
> bestowed upon the faithful the fire of your glory,
> sanctify + this new fire, we pray,
> and grant that,
> by these paschal celebrations,
> we may be so inflamed with heavenly desires,
> that with minds made pure
> we may attain festivities of unending splendor.
> Through Christ our Lord.

---

[160] See Paul Turner, *Glory in the Cross: Holy Week in the Third Edition of* The Roman Missal (Collegeville, MN: Liturgical Press, 2011), 118.

[161] Roman Missal, Easter Vigil, no. 9.

Candle

That source of all light in the faith, the "fire of glory," inspires us to be "inflamed with heavenly desires," and to "attain festivities of unending splendor." Are these first symbols of the Easter Vigil reigniting your memory of that *dies natalis*, that day of your new birth? If not, perhaps a Pillar of Fire and a Pillar of Cloud may bring even greater clarity.

"After the blessing of the new fire," instructs the Roman Missal, "one of the ministers brings the paschal candle to the Priest, who cuts a cross into the candle with a stylus. Then he makes the Greek letter Alpha above the cross, the letter Omega below, and the four numerals of the current year between the arms of the cross."[162] While we haven't seen candles yet during Lent and the Paschal Triduum, the priest's action of cutting the candle reminds us of the *charac*, or cutting tool, from which we derive the word *character*. Recall that for the apostles and their successors to "do this," that is, confect the Eucharist and present again the sacrifice of the Cross, they rely on the power of sacramental character. This character conforms the receiver to Jesus and His three saving offices, particularly His priesthood, and enables or empowers the recipient to exercise that priesthood. A similar character shows itself at this point in the Vigil, as the priest's stylus serves as a *charac*, making its permanent mark—Christ's mark—on the paschal candle.

As the Missal notes, the priest carves three characters with his *charac*: the cross, the Greek Alpha (A), and the Omega (Ω), which are all symbolic of the universal salvation found in Christ's universal Church. By these marks, the candle is being configured

---

[162] Ibid., no. 11.

to Christ. For, as the cross etched in wax signifies Jesus, so the Alpha and the Omega imprinted in the wax also mark the candle as His own, since He is "the Alpha and the Omega, the beginning and the end" (Rev. 21:6).[163] The priest also inscribes the four numerals of the year around the cross to indicate as well that He is present in time and at all times.

Now that Christ has claimed the candle as His own, a second set of liturgical actions further evokes Christ the true light. "When the cutting of the cross and of the other signs has been completed," the Missal notes, "the Priest may insert five grains of incense into the candle in the form of a cross."[164] To this material action, the priest adds the following words, thus sacramentalizing a hidden reality: "By his holy and glorious wounds, may Christ the Lord guard us and protect us. Amen." The candle, already bearing the marks of Jesus in many other ways, is now "wounded" as He was, the five grains evoking His five wounds.[165]

Still other features of the paschal candle identify it with the glorious Christ, who is history's true Pillar of Fire through the darkness of night. For "effective symbolism," the Church's instructions say, the paschal candle "must be made of wax, never be artificial, be renewed each year, be only one in number, and

---

[163] While the priest makes these various marks, he says at the same time: "Christ yesterday and today, the Beginning and the End, the Alpha and the Omega, all time belongs to him and all the ages. To him be glory and power through every age and for ever. Amen." Roman Missal, Easter Vigil, no. 11.

[164] Roman Missal, Easter Vigil, no. 12.

[165] A permanent altar also resembles Christ in this way, with its surface anointed with the scented, sacred chrism on five locations, the center and four corners (*The Order for the Dedication of an Altar*, no. 49). Like the Paschal Candle, the altar becomes a sacramental sign of Christ.

be of sufficiently large size so that it may evoke the truth that Christ is the light of the world."[166] Because Christ is authentic, never artificial, so, too, His candle must come from natural ingredients. Since our Redeemer brings new life, not old or "recycled" existence, so, too, His sacramental candle must be brand new. Furthermore, as Jesus "alone is the Holy One, he alone is the Lord, he alone is the Most High," so the paschal candle must stand alone, unaccompanied by another competing pillar. And unlike a whimpering, flickering wick, the Son of God is an eternal and immense flame. For this reason, his Passover's Pillar of Fire is necessarily large and bright.

The paschal candle, in all its subtle yet significant details, has become a Pillar of Fire for us to follow over salvation's bridge, but now in a way even more real and salvific than that which guided the Children of Israel. Only a few more preparations are required before we, the new Children of Israel, move out to claim our promised inheritance.

Procession

Where there's smoke there's fire, and in the case of the Easter Vigil, the converse is also true. For along with the Pillar of Fire, we are about to be led as well by a Pillar of Cloud. "Just as the children of Israel were guided at night by a pillar of fire," the Church tells us, "so similarly Christians follow the risen Christ."[167] But if you recall the Israelites' first Passover out of Egypt (and, if you don't, the Liturgy of the Word is about to

---

[166] *Paschalis Sollemnitatis*, no. 82.

[167] Ibid., no. 83.

recount it for us), they were led not only by a Pillar of Fire, but also by a Column of Cloud (Exod. 14:19). Both Pillar and Column are related: the Pillar of Fire is a figure of Jesus, as we've noted, and the Column of Cloud is an image of the Holy Spirit.[168] Thus, following the preparation and blessing of the paschal candle, immediately before the procession sets off, "one of the ministers takes burning coals from the fire and places them in the thurible, and the Priest puts incense into it in the usual way."[169] It all happens in a flash, so it may be easy to miss. This firing up of the thurible is an important detail, for on every other liturgical occasion when incense is used, the server lights conveniently packaged and easily lit charcoals. But on this night—a night unlike any other—the coals from the Easter fire ignite the incense and produce the column of cloud that we follow into the church. It's as if the fire enflames the cloud, just as the cloud followed by the Israelites was a "fiery cloud" through which the Lord cast "upon the Egyptian force a glance that threw it into a panic" (Exod. 14:24). Our own demonic pursuers are likewise about to panic.

Now that the candle and incense—or, more accurately, the Pillar of Fire and Column of Cloud—are ready, the procession may begin. But this procession is not the same in kind as our Good Friday movement "as if in procession" to adore the cross. Rather, since history's greatest bridge is about to be crossed, such a moment demands an orderly, beautiful, and cosmetic procession of the faithful. Hear how the Missal describes the process of entering the Promised Land: "The Deacon or, if there is no

---

[168] Clouds, rain, dew, and shadows are frequent figures, even theophanies, of the Holy Spirit in Sacred Scripture. See CCC 697.

[169] Roman Missal, Easter Vigil, no. 13.

Deacon, another suitable minister, takes the paschal candle and a procession forms. The thurifer with the smoking thurible precedes the Deacon or other minister who carries the paschal candle. After them follows the Priest with the ministers and the people, all holding in their hands unlit candles."[170] These liturgical elements and the order in which they proceed recall and fulfill what was at one time anticipated thousands of years ago by the Israelites coming out of Egypt. As Moses led the Chosen People out of the land of slavery and death into a new life of freedom, they were guided by a Column of Cloud and Pillar of Fire. Accordingly then, we, too, follow cloud and fire, behind our priest and leader, out of the darkness of night into a new world beautifully lit by Christ.

But more than merely replicating the Israelites' Passover, our procession more properly follows Christ's passage from death to life. "The Passover Vigil," instructs the Church, "in which the Hebrews kept watch for the Lord's passover which was to free them from slavery to Pharaoh, is an annual commemoration. It prefigured the true Pasch of Christ that was to come, the night that is of true liberation, in which 'destroying the bonds of death, Christ rose as victor from the depths.'"[171] But we don't simply acknowledge this reality in silence. Holy Saturday has now passed into Easter, and our voices announce the very truth of Christ's victory as we enter the church building. The deacon or minister carrying the candle (the priest—Moses—does *not* carry the candle, but follows it at the head of his people) stops at three points during the procession: at the church entrance, at the midpoint during the procession up the church's center aisle,

---

[170] Ibid., no. 15.

[171] *Paschalis Sollemnitatis*, no. 79.

and in the sanctuary before the altar. At each of these points he sings, "The Light of Christ," to which we all respond, "Thanks be to God," as we light our own smaller candles and brightness slowly spreads throughout the church's interior. These smaller acclamations, which take place during the procession, though, pale in comparison to the paschal praise about to be heaped upon the candle in the *Exsultet*.

Easter Proclamation (Exsultet)

When the procession of cloud, fire, Moses, and Chosen People reaches the heart of the Promised Land—that is, when thurifer, candles, priest, and People of God approach the church sanctuary—the paschal candle stands in place in the middle of the sanctuary or near the ambo. At this point, each of the lights in the formerly darkened church are turned on—as if the paschal candle, now arrived at last, has ignited every other light.[172] We have already acclaimed the paschal candle's greatness during the procession out of darkness and into the light. And now that its light floods the church, these overtures give way to the full-throated symphony of praise as the deacon prepares to sing the *Exsultet*.

The Vigil's night, fire, candle, and procession (which are the first parts of what the Roman Missal calls the *Lucernarium*) render Jesus' Resurrection from the dead present and active in visible signs and symbols. The *Exsultet* (the final element of the *Lucernarium*) does the same, in part by other perceptible symbols, but principally in its poetic, sung verse. The author of the

---

[172] Roman Missal, Easter Vigil, no. 17; also Turner, *Glory in the Cross*, 127.

Exsultet—the Church—explains that the purpose of this composition is to tell "by means of a great poetic text the whole Easter mystery, placed in the context of the economy of salvation."[173] In other words, the story told in sacramental signs by the fire, candle, and procession is the same account sung poetically by the *Exsultet*. For instance, the *Exsultet* begins by recounting that first Passover, where God "led our forebears, Israel's children, from slavery in Egypt and made them pass dry-shod through the Red Sea." It then joyfully proclaims that Christ has now broken the "prison-bars of death," the reason for our entire being and the grand purpose of the Triduum. Next, in the *Exsultet*, the Church exclaims a litany of praise and wonder:

> O wonder of your humble care for us!
> O love, O charity beyond all telling,
> to ransom a slave you gave away your Son!
> O truly necessary sin of Adam,
> destroyed completely by the Death of Christ!
> O happy fault
> that earned so great, so glorious a Redeemer!
> O truly blessed night,
> worthy alone to know the time and hour
> when Christ rose from the underworld!

This "happy fault," or *felix culpa*, expresses precisely the unfathomable paradox of salvation: a God who becomes man saves a people who have (as it turns out) happily fallen so that humans might become divine. The enigmatic expression has caught the attention of many pious minds through the years, as it should ours today. Why, we should ask, is our fall a happy one? Because,

---

[173] *Paschalis Sollemnitatis*, no. 84.

the *Exsultet* says, it earned for us a divine redeemer that gives us life now in greater abundance than our first parents ever had. Monsignor Reynold Hillenbrand (1905–1975), a great promotor, pastor, and teacher of the liturgy, explains why our fall was so felicitous: "The truth is simple: the world, with all its present disabilities, is now more glorious, is now more fraught with possibilities for our divine life than paradise would have been.... We can become greater saints, than we could if Adam had never sinned and Eden had remained."[174] Happy fault indeed!

The *Exsultet* next presents one of its more beautiful images: that of the mother bee and her hive, collaborating with human hands in forming the paschal candle. The deacon sings:

> On this, your night of grace, O holy Father,
> accept this candle, a solemn offering,
> the work of bees and of your servants' hands,
> an evening sacrifice of praise,
> this gift from your most holy Church.
> But now we know the praises of this pillar,
> which glowing fire ignites for God's honor,

---

[174] Monsignor Hillenbrand continues with a further explanation: "Doubtlessly, one of the reasons we are such dull, routine Christians and have so little effect upon the world is that we have no sense of this, no sense of our newness in Christ. We are so much engrossed with the riddling effects of the first sin. We sense the collapse, not the restoration. We sense the Fall, not the lifting up. We sense the ancient enthrallment, not the release into the new glorious freedom, the freedom of the sons of God. Our thinking is so pre-Incarnation, if I can put it that way. We direct our attention to the lost Paradise rather than to the infinitely more wonderful, though immensely more difficult, world that we have now." Proceedings from the 1948 National Liturgical Week, "The New Man in Christ," August 2–6, Boston, 33.

> a fire into many flames divided,
> yet never dimmed by sharing of its light,
> for it is fed by melting wax,
> drawn out by mother bees
> to build a torch so precious.

The common honeybee is not so common after all, as it brings with it numerous symbolic insights. The hive's pure wax joins with the fire of Christ to announce God the Father's new *Fiat lux*, the light of a new creation. The bees thus praise the risen Christ according to their own gifts. By their wax, they hum (or buzz) along with the Church's Te Deum prayer, offered in the Office of Readings on Sundays and Solemnities: "You are God: we praise you; You are the Lord: we acclaim you; You are the eternal Father: All creation worships you!" The bees also work as a perfect natural society, each working toward a single end for their mother, or queen. The colony thus reflects the Mother Church and her members. St. Augustine, in fact, likens the Church's newly baptized to bees: "I speak to you who have just been reborn in baptism, my little children in Christ, you who are the new offspring of the Church, gift of the Father, proof of Mother Church's fruitfulness. All of you who stand fast in the Lord are a holy seed, a new colony of bees, the very flower of our ministry and fruit of our toil, my joy and my crown."[175]

The swarm of symbols we learned about from the *Exsultet's* praise for the honeybee carries the song to its concluding theme: Christ's saving victory. "How do I love thee?" the Church may well be asking Jesus at this point. "Let me count the ways!"

---

[175] St. Augustine, Office of Readings from Sunday within the Octave of Easter, vol. II, 635–636.

Through song, the Bride of Christ spills over in her love for Christ in a variety of ways. Such infinite variety in the *Exsultet* is a reflection of the complex yet discernable symbolism we find in the Easter Vigil in general. This same symbolism that fills the *Exsultet*, the Church's love song to God, also emerges from the Church's desire to tell the love story that inspired the song: for, like the *Lucernarium*, the Liturgy of the Word also sheds light on the Paschal Mystery unfolding before us in the Easter Vigil.

Liturgy of the Word

The Liturgy of the Word forms the second part of the Easter Vigil, revealing in Scripture the same glorious Paschal Mystery presented to our eyes in the *Lucernarium*'s blessing of the fire and the candle and the procession, and sung to our ears in its *Exsultet*. But the Liturgy of the Word also marks a change in the liturgy's tone. For, if "spectacle" best describes the Vigil thus far, "meditation" defines the readings from the Scriptures: "They give the account of the outstanding deeds of the history of salvation, which the faithful are helped to meditate calmly upon."[176] To direct our meditations, the Lectionary offers a tapestry interwoven with narrative, psalms, and prayers. There are nine readings in the Liturgy of the Word for the Easter Vigil, seven from the Old Testament, a New Testament reading from St. Paul, and the Gospel. Each Old Testament reading is followed by a psalm, and each ends with a prayer by the priest in the name of the people. The readings include:

Genesis 1:1–2:2 — on the creation of the cosmos

Genesis 22:1–18 — on Abraham's sacrifice of Isaac

---

[176] *Paschalis Sollemnitatis*, no. 85.

Exodus 14:15–15:1—on the passage of the Chosen
People through the Red Sea

Isaiah 54:5–14—on the New Jerusalem

Isaiah 55:1–11—on the salvation that is offered to all

Baruch 3:9–15—on the fountain of wisdom

Ezekiel 36:16–28—on the creation of a new heart
and a new spirit[177]

Ideally, each of these readings is included in this Mass "so that
the character of the Vigil, which demands an extended period of
time, may be preserved."[178] But if "more serious pastoral circumstances demand it," the number of readings may be reduced to at
least three, with selections from both the Law and the Prophets,
but always including the story of the Chosen People's first exodus
out of Egypt from Exodus 14.[179] If the people are to "meditate
[upon] the wonderful works that the Lord God wrought for his
people from the earliest times," then these events must be proclaimed. Only then can the Church, "'beginning with Moses and
all the prophets,' explain Christ's paschal mystery."[180]

The Vigil's readings from the Law (Genesis 1, Genesis 22,
and Exodus 14) feature foreshadowings that find fulfillment in
Christ. This "typological" manner of scriptural interpretation
sees in persons, things, and events of the Old Testament types
and prefigurements of Jesus, His Church, and His sacraments.
What we have seen already in our discussion of the *Lucernarium*
is now accounted for by Scripture: the Pillar of Fire and the

---

[177] See Roman Missal, Easter Vigil, nos. 23–30.

[178] Ibid., no. 20.

[179] Ibid., no. 21; also *Paschalis Sollemnitatis*, no. 85.

[180] *Paschalis Sollemnitatis*, no. 85.

Column of Cloud leading the Chosen People out of Egypt in the Old Testament foreshadowed and prefigured Jesus and the Holy Spirit leading a new Chosen People out of this world's slavery and sin. This particular typological interpretation is only one of a multitude of examples contained in these three readings, and each resolves itself in one person: Jesus. "All the Old Covenant prefigurations," says the *Catechism*, "find their fulfillment in Christ Jesus" (CCC 1223). The second-century St. Melito of Sardis gives some paschal-specific examples:

> It is he who endured every kind of suffering in all those who foreshadowed him. In Abel he was slain, in Isaac bound, in Jacob exiled, in Joseph sold, in Moses exposed to die. He was sacrificed in the Passover lamb, persecuted in David, dishonored in the prophets.... He is the mute lamb, the slain lamb born of Mary, the fair ewe. He was seized from the flock, dragged off to be slaughtered, sacrificed in the evening, and buried at night.[181]

An early fourth-century author known to us today as Pseudo-Chrysostom likewise sees Christ's reality anticipated in Old Testament types:

> In an imperfect and transitory way, the types and images of the past prefigured the perfect and eternal reality which has now been revealed.... Correctly understood, its very name [i.e., "Passover"] shows why this is our greatest feast. It is called the Passover because, when he was striking down the firstborn, the destroying angel passed over the

---

[181] St. Melito of Sardis, Office of Readings for Thursday of Holy Week, vol. II, 459.

houses of the Hebrews, but it is even more true to say that he passes over us, for he does so once and for all when we are raised up by Christ to eternal life.[182]

When we listen to the readings in the Liturgy of the Word, then, we should direct our meditations to the spiritual realities that underlie the types and figures of salvation history. In this way, we can more clearly see in salvation history how God has been at work for thousands of years waiting to receive us over Christ's paschal bridge.

But even in the Liturgy of the Word, and apart from its many Old Testament texts, the Easter Vigil is unique. As a punctuation mark on the Old Testament series of readings, the Liturgy of the Word includes the singing of the Gloria, during which bells are rung and the altar's candles lit. The Opening Prayer, or Collect, for the Easter Vigil is then prayed. Next there is read "an exhortation from the apostles on baptism as an insertion into Christ's paschal mystery."[183] This "insertion" into Christ's Paschal Mystery is exactly what will take place by water, oil, and bread in the next part of the Vigil, the celebration of the Sacraments of Initiation.

What comes next is, as far as the Liturgy of the Word is concerned, the moment we've all be waiting for: even as the darkness gave way first to the Easter fire and then to the paschal candle, so the shadows give way to reality as the Gospel proclaims Jesus' Resurrection from the dead (Matt. 28:1–10; Mark 16:1–7; Luke 24:1–12). Lest anyone miss the significance

---

[182] Pseudo-Chrysostom, Office of Readings for Monday, Easter Week II, vol. II, 644–645.

[183] *Paschalis Sollemnitatis*, no. 87.

of the Gospel reading (perhaps the late hour of night and the "calmness" of meditation have begun to take a toll), the liturgy once again signifies the reading's importance in a variety of noteworthy ways. For example, at the bishop's celebration of the Vigil, a deacon comes before him prior to the Gospel Alleluia and says, "Most Reverend Father, I bring you a message of great joy, the message of Alleluia."[184] Next, the bishop, or the priest in the parish, stands and intones the Alleluia. Nowhere else throughout the Church year is the priest asked to do so. But on this night, when Christ our priest rises from the dead, Christ's priest rises to sing the Alleluia.[185] And not only does the priest sing the Alleluia, but he sings it three times, "raising his voice by a step each time, with all repeating it," the rising pitch of his voice announcing Christ rising in glory. By each of these sacramental details, the substance and reality of the Gospel's words — the Father's Word — reveal the victorious Christ more audibly and powerfully.

The Easter Vigil's Liturgy of the Word, the second part of the Vigil, announces in meditative yet powerful ways the resurrected Christ. From the first verses on creation in Genesis to the new creation accounts in the Gospels, their contents enable attentive ears to hear and even reverberate with the divine word. "The light of the Only-begotten has shone on us," says St. Cyril of Alexandria, "and we have been transformed into the Word, the source of all life."[186] Hearing, too, is believing.

---

[184] *Ceremonial of Bishops*, no. 352.

[185] "If necessary, the psalmist intones the Alleluia." Roman Missal, Easter Vigil, no. 34; also *Paschalis Sollemnitatis*, no. 87.

[186] St. Cyril of Alexandria, Office of Readings for the Sixth Sunday of Easter, vol. II, 873.

Conclusion

Entering the Promised Land takes place in stages. It begins in darkness illumined by fire. A candle and cloud direct the journey. We enter a new Jerusalem that welcomes us with light, poetry, and song. And by meditating on the Word, we sense the victory of our service as "little bridge builders" in God's divine plan. But the *Lucernarium*, its *Exsultet*, and the Liturgy of the Word lead us still further along our Easter journey as we prepare to celebrate the sacraments of baptism, confirmation, and the Eucharist — the far shore of the Paschal Mystery.

In Brief

+ Just as He has done in all of the Triduum's liturgies, the victorious Christ comes to meet us and lead us from death to life through sacramental signs and symbols.

+ The darkness of Easter night signifies the ignorance, fear, and death of the world of sin, while the burning fire in its midst radiates the new warmth, light, and life of Christ.

+ Engraved with the Sign of the Cross, marked with the Alpha and the Omega, bearing five grains of incense, the paschal candle symbolizes Christ our Light, the one radiant Bearer of the new creation's light and life.

+ The Chosen People were led out of Egypt by Moses, their leader, who followed a Column of Cloud by day and a Pillar of Fire by night. In so doing, they anticipated Jesus' Paschal Mystery. Today, God's Chosen People similarly follow the thurible's smoke and the paschal candle's flame behind their priest, passing over into the church building, the image of the new and eternal Promised Land.

✦ What the *Lucernarium*'s fire, candle, and procession reveal in symbols, the *Exsultet* proclaims in poetry and song. Our Fall, once a cause of death and sadness, has become by God's power the source of joy and happiness, for Christ has redeemed us and drawn us even closer to God than our first parents ever were in Eden.

✦ The Liturgy of the Word provides nine readings, along with psalms and prayers, that foster a meditative hearing of the saving works of God in salvation history. Seeing in the Old Testament figures the future redeeming work of Jesus, hearing the bells rung during the Gloria, and singing along with the priest, who, on this night alone, intones the triple Alleluia, renders the Word of the Trinity audible to the fallen yet restored human ear.

THE NEXT TIME YOU ENTER THE EASTER VIGIL

✦ Notice as many details as possible. Jesus draws us upward through the smell of incense, the heat of the Easter fire, the song of the *Exsultet*, the sight of a sea of small flames, the movement in procession — and more.

✦ Meditate beforehand on the text of the *Exsultet*. When hearing it at the Easter Vigil, consider carefully and prayerfully the poetic images throughout the text.

✦ During the Liturgy of the Word, notice in the Old Testament persons and events the many ways in which God has been preparing the world for Christ's Paschal Mystery, and how you are able to share in it more profoundly now than any before Him: Adam, Moses, Abraham, Isaac, Isaiah. God's Old Testament People are shadows of you, the reality.

8

How to Be Re-Created:
The Easter Vigil's Sacraments

✠

Our Redeemer's visible presence has passed into the sacraments.

—St. Leo the Great[187]

If you had to choose, would you rather walk alongside the historical Jesus in the Promised Land, listen to His preaching, and be fed and healed by His holy, human hands—or would you prefer to encounter Him in the Mass, hear and reply to His voice in liturgical prayer, and receive Him in holy Communion from the hands of a priest? It may seem a strange proposition, but its answer figured prominently for many who sought to encounter Christ in His fullness.

The 1918 book *The Spirit of the Liturgy* by Romano Guardini (1885–1968) was one of the most influential works on the sacred liturgy in the twentieth century. In a chapter on "The Style of the Liturgy," this German priest and theologian addresses this same question. More than one person, he suggests, would

---

[187] St. Leo the Great, Office of Readings for Friday, Easter Week VI, vol. II, 937.

exchange theological knowledge of Jesus or our liturgical encounter with Him "if as against that it were permitted to him to watch Jesus walking about the streets or to hear the tone in which He addresses a disciple. More than one would be willing to sacrifice the most beautiful liturgical prayer, if in exchange he might meet Christ face to face and speak to Him from the bottom of his heart."[188] In asserting that the faithful would prefer Christ as He appeared during His thirty-three years on earth, Guardini addresses a misunderstanding of many in his day—namely, that the liturgy lacked the same substance as seeing Christ in the flesh.

For these, Guardini surmised, the liturgy and the sacraments were an imperfect and ineffective way to relate to Jesus. Indeed, some saw the Church's sacred rituals as obstacles to encountering Christ, and not an indispensable means for meeting Him. But such confusion only weakens one's ability to come to Christ and receive His grace in the present age. True, while each of the baptized ought to converse personally with our Lord, speaking and engaging Him according to his particular needs, temperaments, and circumstances, our full conformity to Christ must also include liturgical and sacramental engagement. For the sacred liturgy is, in its unique, God-given way, filled with the real Jesus. Sacramental worship is not an empty shell of Christ: to celebrate the sacramental liturgy is to encounter Christ Himself.

The paschal bridge to heaven, then, passes through the sacraments since, as St. Leo the Great says, "Our Redeemer's visible

---

[188]Romano Guardini, *The Spirit of the Liturgy* (New York: Crossroad, 1998), 50.

presence has passed into the sacraments."[189] This sacramental system suits Him perfectly, for He Himself is a sacrament of the Father. As he explains to St. Philip, "Whoever has seen me has seen the Father.... I am in the Father and the Father is in me" (John 14:9–10). In other words, to have seen or heard or touched Jesus was to see and hear and touch the otherwise undetectable Father. For his part, St. Paul sees Jesus as "the image of the invisible God" (Col. 1:15). Summing up these verses, St. Augustine simply says, "There is no other mystery [i.e., sacrament] of God, except Christ" (see CCC 774).

Therefore, as the Father is reflected in the Son, so the Son is reflected in the sacraments. In our current Age of the Church, the victorious Christ—having suffered, died, risen, and ascended—comes to us and we to Him principally in the sacraments. Christ, who is the sacrament of God the Father, saves us through His Church's sacraments. The *Catechism* explains, He "manifests, makes present, and communicates his work of salvation through the liturgy of his Church, 'until he comes' (1 Cor. 11:26).... Christ now lives and acts in and with his Church, in a new way appropriate to this new age. He acts through the sacraments" (CCC 1076). Short of martyrdom, we participate in Christ's saving work to the highest degree through the sacraments.

"This is something amazing and unheard of!" exclaims the fourth-century *Jerusalem Catechesis*. "It was not we who actually died, were buried and rose again. We only did these things symbolically, but we have been saved in actual fact. It is Christ who was crucified, who was buried and who rose again, and all this has

---

[189] St. Leo the Great, Office of Readings for Friday, Easter Week VI, vol. II, 937.

been attributed to us. We share in his sufferings symbolically and gain salvation in reality."[190] Inspired by these words, it's worth repeating: completing the paschal bridge passes through the sacraments. No "fork in the road" to heaven exists, one through Jesus, another through sacraments—both are the same. For this reason, the liturgy of liturgies that celebrates Christ's victory does so by means of the sacraments, which signal and present that same victory. For, following the Easter Vigil's solemn procession into the church building, the singing of the Easter Proclamation, and the Liturgy of the Word, the Church initiates new members into her fold by the sacraments of baptism, confirmation, and the Eucharist. In these rites, "we are inserted into the Paschal Mystery of Christ," in which we die with Him, are buried with Him, and rise with Him—and reign with Him.[191] This chapter will offer spiritual insights into these three sacraments of initiation, looking beyond the outward signs to their inward realities. St. Ambrose tells his newly initiated, "You were told before not to believe only what you saw."[192] We, too, wish to see through the symbols to Christ within, for sacraments are images of the invisible Christ. As we have done throughout the book, we will take as our starting point the rites themselves as found in the Roman Missal and rely afterward on the spiritual insights of the Church Fathers, particularly as the Church presents them to us in the Office of Readings.

---

[190] *Jerusalem Catechesis*, Office of Readings for Thursday within the Octave of Easter, vol. II, 597. The author of the quoted text is believed to be either St. Cyril of Jerusalem (bishop from 350 to 386) or his successor, John II (bishop from 387 to 417).

[191] *Paschalis Sollemnitatis*, no. 80.

[192] St. Ambrose, Office of Readings for Wednesday of the Fifteenth Week in Ordinary Time, vol. III, 496.

Sacrament of Baptism

The Fathers of the Second Vatican Council desired to restore the ancient catechumenate, a process of forming adults "who, after hearing the mystery of Christ proclaimed, consciously and freely seek the living God and enter the way of faith and conversion as the Holy Spirit opens their hearts. By God's help they will be strengthened spiritually during their preparation and at the proper time will receive the sacraments fruitfully."[193] Such a restoration signals the Church's desire to see the sacraments as a central element of Christian life, and since the Easter Vigil is the central moment of liturgical life, it also serves as a fitting throne for these sacraments. Thus, when these adults are properly prepared to be initiated, the Easter Vigil provides the natural (and supernatural) occasion for reception of these sacraments, starting with baptism.[194] Each element of the baptismal liturgy — from the procession to the font to the reception of the baptismal candle — speaks to this same fruitfulness for those about to take the plunge into death and new life.

Procession to the Font

The baptismal liturgy begins with the calling of the candidates, whether they are adults or infants. If the baptism occurs in a baptistery apart from the sanctuary, a procession forms and is led by the paschal candle.[195] The candidates are accompanied by

---

[193] *Rite of Christian Initiation of Adults* (RCIA), no. 1; also *Sacrosanctum Concilium*, no. 64.

[194] See *Paschalis Sollemnitatis*, no. 7.

[195] Roman Missal, Easter Vigil, no. 39; also RCIA, no. 219.

their godparents, the priest, and the saints, whose litany is sung during the procession. In a homily addressed to those who had been recently baptized, St. Cyril of Jerusalem (d. 386) describes to his candidates how their procession was anticipated by Old Testament types fulfilled by Christ: "As Moses was appointed to lead his afflicted people from Egypt, so Christ came to deliver the people of the world who were overcome by sin. That tyrant of old pursued the ancient Jewish people as far as the sea, and here and now the devil, bold and shameless, the source of all evil, followed you up to the waters of salvation."[196] Thus, as that first Passover featured the leading candle, an "angel of God" (Exod. 14:19), the guiding hand of Moses, and the assembly of the people, so now the true Passover sees similar elements: candle, warrior saints, priest leader, and people destined for freedom.

Blessing of Holy Water

When the procession arrives at the font or baptistery, the priest blesses its holy water. The formula for blessing tells of the history of water in the story of salvation — and how it has become sacramental water for us today. After beginning with a clear statement of water's symbolic power — "O God, who by invisible power accomplish a wondrous effect through sacramental signs"[197] — the prayer recounts the place of water in "the first moments of creation," then in the "outpouring of the flood," followed by the passing through the waters of the Red Sea, leading to Jesus' baptism by John "in the waters of the Jordan," recalling

---

[196] St. Cyril of Jerusalem, in Yarnold, *Awe-Inspiring Rites*, 71.

[197] Roman Missal, Easter Vigil, no. 46.

water streaming "from his side along with blood," and concluding with the great commission to baptize all nations. Baptismal water ceases to be merely natural water: it is now supernatural water, a "living, leaping water, welling up for those who are worthy," as St. Cyril of Jerusalem (d. 386) says.[198]

One ingredient of baptism's life-giving water is the Holy Spirit. In the story of the Exodus, the Column of Cloud appears illuminated and fiery (Exod. 14:20, 24) — Pillar and Column, Son and Spirit, truly united in saving God's people. Similarly, during the blessing of the font, the priest may lower the paschal candle into the water once or three times. Thus, symbolically, Christ enters the water before we do. As He had done before, so now the Pillar of Fire shows the way to God's new Chosen People through the font's deadly waters. But it is not only Christ who enters the water; as the text prayed during the lowering of the candles also suggests, the action represents an epiclesis, or calling down of the Holy Spirit. With "radiant cloud" in hand, the priest asks, "May the power of the Holy Spirit, O Lord, we pray, come down through your Son into the fullness of this font."[199] The Syrian St. Theodore of Mopsuestia (d. 428) says of this blessed river of life, "You are not baptized in ordinary water, but in the water of second birth. Now ordinary water cannot become this other thing except by the coming of the Holy Spirit. Consequently, the bishop beforehand pronounces a prescribed form of words, asking God to let the grace of the Holy Spirit come upon the water and make it capable of begetting this awesome birth, making it a womb for

---

[198] St. Cyril of Jerusalem, Office of Readings for Monday, Easter Week VII, vol. II, 967.

[199] Roman Missal, Easter Vigil, no. 46.

sacramental birth."[200] In either image—candle as guiding Pillar of Fire or as sanctifying Column of Cloud, Son and Spirit are present and active to save us through extraordinary water.

Renunciation of Satan

Now that the font and its water are ready to receive us (or, as St. Theodore suggests above, *conceive* us), we, too, must make some final preparations. Before being admitted into the font, the candidates themselves have a few things to admit:[201]

Priest: Do you renounce Satan?

Elect: I do.

Priest: And all his works?

Elect: I do.

Priest: And all his empty show?

Elect: I do.[202]

Many of the Church Fathers had their candidates for baptism sacramentalize their rejection of the enemy not only in their words, but also in their bodies by facing the west, that place on the earth at which the sun disappears and gives way to the arid darkness of night before turning back to the illuminating waters of the new day about to dawn. St. Cyril of Jerusalem, for example, explains, "You faced westward ... and renounced Satan as though to his face.... [Y]ou trample underfoot your entire covenant with him, and abrogate

---

[200] St. Theodore of Mopsuestia, in Yarnold, *Awe-Inspiring Rites*, 185.

[201] The faithful may join the elect in renewing their own baptismal promises, or else these follow the celebration of confirmation. See Roman Missal, Easter Vigil, nos. 49, 55.

[202] Roman Missal, Easter Vigil, no. 55; also *RCIA*, no. 224. The Roman Missal includes a second formula for the renunciation.

your former treaty with Hell.... When you turned from west to east, the region of light, you symbolized this change of allegiance."[203] In the liturgy generally, and during the Paschal Triduum especially, no external sign or symbol lacks importance. Even the directions on the compass point us away from sin and toward God.

Anointing with the Oil of Catechumens

But, as you can imagine, renouncing Satan to his face—some traditions even spit in his face[204]—before turning your back on him is not without its risks, even if the rewards are great. For this reason, the candidates are next anointed with the Oil of Catechumens to engage the Devil in battle.[205] Only a few days earlier, when the bishop blessed the Oil of Catechumens during Holy Week's Chrism Mass, he informed us about its saving and strengthening purpose.

O God, strength and protection of your people, who have made the oil you created a sign of strength, graciously

---

[203] Yarnold, *Awe-Inspiring Rites*, 70, 74.

[204] See ibid., 19.

[205] "If the anointing of the adults with the Oil of Catechumens has not taken place, as part of the immediately preparatory rites beforehand, it occurs at this moment" (Roman Missal, Easter Vigil, no. 48). In the Dioceses of the United States, however, the *National Statutes on the Catechumenate* from the United States Conference of Catholic Bishops directs that the anointing of adults is omitted at the Easter Vigil and is reserved for the Period of the Catechumenate and the Period of Purification and Enlightenment (see *RCIA*, no. 33.7; also *National Statutes on the Catechumenate*, no. 16). If infants are to be baptized at the Easter Vigil, they are anointed at a suitable time before the Easter Vigil Mass begins (*The Order of Baptism of Children*, no. 28).

bless + this oil, and grant courage to the catechumens who will be anointed with it, so that, receiving divine wisdom and power, they may understand more deeply the Gospel of your Christ, they may undertake with a generous heart the labors of the Christian life, and, made worthy of adoption as your sons and daughters, they may rejoice to be born anew and to live in your Church. Through Christ our Lord.[206]

Strength, courage, power: these essential weapons are conveyed to the candidates before they grapple with the Leviathan beneath the waves of the font. St. Ambrose will remind his victorious neophytes, "We arrived at the baptistery. You went in, and were anointed. You were rubbed with oil like an athlete, Christ's athlete, as though in preparation for an earthly wrestling match, and you agreed to take on your opponent."[207]

St. John Chrysostom makes even clearer the death-dealing Devil who awaits those who have betrayed his authority in the water:

Now the bishop knows that the Enemy is enraged and is sharpening his teeth, going around like a roaring lion, seeing that the former victims of his tyranny have suddenly defected. Renouncing him, they have changed their allegiance and publicly enlisted with Christ. It is for this reason that the bishop anoints you on your forehead and marks you with the seal, to make the

---

[206] *The Order of Blessing the Oil of Catechumens and of the Sick and of Consecrating the Chrism*, no. 22.

[207] St. Ambrose, in Yarnold, *Awe-Inspiring Rites*, 101–102.

devil turn away his eyes. He does not dare to look at you directly because he sees the light blazing from your head and blinding his eyes. From that day onwards you will confront him in battle, and this is why the bishop anoints you as athletes of Christ before leading you into the spiritual arena.[208]

Satan wants to kill us, body, soul, and spirit, but now our training has paid off: boot camp is done, and we're ready to take to the field of battle. And while he'll continue to tempt us and regain our allegiance throughout our lives, baptism turns us from him to God in the most powerful way.

Profession of Faith

On the doorstep of the Red Sea—that is, the baptismal font —those about to go beneath the water now profess their faith in Father, Son, and Holy Spirit:

Priest: Do you believe in God,
the Father almighty,
Creator of heaven and earth?

Elect: I do.

Priest: Do you believe in Jesus Christ, his only Son, our Lord,
who was born of the Virgin Mary,
suffered death and was buried,
rose again from the dead
and is seated at the right hand of the Father?

Elect: I do.

---

[208] St. John Chrysostom, in Yarnold, *Awe-Inspiring Rites*, 160.

Priest: Do you believe in the Holy Spirit,
      the holy catholic Church,
      the communion of saints,
      the forgiveness of sins,
      the resurrection of the body,
      and life everlasting?
Elect: I do.

Like the renunciation before it, a cardinal point of the compass adds efficacy to the spoken word. In some rites, the eastward direction was employed to emphasize one's profession of the Son. "Atonement comes to you from the east," Origen of Alexandria (d. 253) says. "From the east comes the one whose name is Dayspring, he who is mediator between God and men. You are invited then to look always to the east: it is there that the sun of righteousness rises for you, it is there that the light is always being born for you."[209] God, through His Church, deals with us according to our natures. Both bodies and spirits, we come to know, to encounter, and to live through contact with outward signs and symbols found in ordinary objects such as candles, love poems such as the *Exsultet*, simple actions such as anointing with oil, and the points on a compass—all of these symbols help us encounter Christ, who wins our atonement.

But now that the moment has arrived, there is one more ordinary object we must immerse ourselves in to find Christ. The enraged Devil has his teeth sharpened, we are covered in the oil of strength, and the Son is appearing to shine upon us over the horizon. Let the games begin: let us enter the font.

---

[209] Origen, Office of Readings for Monday, Lent Week IV, vol. II, 287.

Baptism

Baptism goes by many names: gift, grace, anointing, enlightenment, clothing, bath, seal (see CCC 1216). Many of these invisible realities turn visible in the font. First, since in baptism we are "washed clean,"[210] the font resembles a bath. Second, because our immersion buries us with Christ "into death,"[211] the font symbolizes a tomb. Third, as the source of "life of newborn children,"[212] the font appears as Mother Church's womb. The Easter season's Office of Readings teaches that "We men are conceived twice: to the human body we owe our first conception, to the divine Spirit, our second."[213] Truly, "newness" might best summarize the Easter Vigil's features: new fire, new candle, new holy water, and, as we emerge from that same font, new Christians.

Our newness comes from the Trinity, author of all creation—old or new. At the creation of the world, recall, God the Father spoke his Word while the mighty Spirit hovered over the waters (see Gen. 1:1). Our creation from the heart of the Trinity made us creatures in God's own image and likeness (Gen. 1:26). Now, at our re-creation, the priest baptizes us "In the name of the Father, and of the Son, and of the Holy Spirit" as he immerses us with water or pours it over our heads. The image and likeness wounded by sin is now restored—and even made more brilliant than before.

---

[210] From the Prayer of Blessing of Baptismal Water, Roman Missal, Easter Vigil, no. 46.

[211] Ibid.

[212] Ibid.

[213] Didymus of Alexandria, Office of Readings for Monday, Easter Week VI, vol. II, 883.

White Garment

As the freshly washed souls, risen and born anew, emerge from the far side of the font, their bodies symbolize their new existence by donning new clothes: the pure-white alb. In handing the neophytes their new vesture, the priest reminds them that they have "become a new creation and have clothed [them]selves in Christ," and to keep these sacramental garments unstained until reaching heaven's judgment. After this vesting, St. Ambrose tells his neophytes, "You were to approach the altar. You began to draw near. The angels looked down and saw you coming. They saw the natural human state, until recently soiled with the gloom and squalor of sin, suddenly shine out brilliantly. This led them to say: 'Who is this that is coming up from the wilderness in white?' The angels, then, also stand and marvel."[214] Baptism is truly a far cry on a far shore from looking the fallen angels in the face. Now, as we wipe the water from our eyes, we see God's angels look us in the face and marvel at our brilliance—a brilliance that returns us, once again, to the light of Christ!

Baptismal Candle

The final element of the baptismal liturgy is the reception of the baptismal candle. It is lit by the godparent from the freshly cut paschal candle and placed in the hands of the newly baptized. Then the priest says to the newly minted Christians, "You have been enlightened by Christ. Walk always as children of the light and keep the flame of faith alive in your hearts. When the Lord

---

[214] St. Ambrose, in Yarnold, *Awe-Inspiring Rites*, no. 129.

comes, may you go out to meet him with all the saints in the heavenly kingdom."[215] St. Gregory of Nazianzus (d. 389) said similarly of life's procession to God, "The lamps which you will light symbolize the torchlight procession in the next world, in which our shining, virgin souls will meet the bridegroom with the shining lights of faith."[216] The Passover to the far side of heaven nears its destination along with the paschal candle and the end of the baptismal liturgy.

Sacrament of Confirmation

All of the newfound realities of baptism — new life, strength, grace, character, purity, enlightenment — are pushed up a notch by the second of the initiation sacraments, confirmation. Following baptism by water, the vesting in the white garment, and the passing of the lighted candle, the newly baptized return from the baptistery to the sanctuary so that they and the Church can "confirm" what has just occurred.[217] In many parishes, the newly baptized are joined at this point by the distantly baptized — those who were baptized Catholic as infants but were not confirmed as

---

[215] *RCIA*, no. 230.

[216] Gregory of Nazianzus, in Yarnold, *Awe-Inspiring Rites*, 34.

[217] If infants (or those beneath the age of reason) have been baptized, these receive a post-baptismal anointing with sacred chrism. Not itself the sacrament of confirmation, this anointing on the crown of the head prays that "As Christ was anointed Priest, Prophet, and King, so may you live always as a member of his body, sharing everlasting life" (Rite of Baptism for One Child, 98). Eventually, the sacrament of confirmation will be celebrated for this group at or soon after the age of discretion (See *Code of Canon Law*, Canon 891).

adolescents (which is the practice for the Latin Church), and by those who were baptized in a non-Catholic Christian communities (e.g., Lutheran or Presbyterian) who now desire to enter into the full communion of the Catholic Church. In each case, the sacrament of confirmation *confirms* baptism, whenever that baptism had been received.

One of the knottiest questions that those learning the Catholic Faith must untie concerns the nature of confirmation. Some see it as a second-rate sequel of baptism. For others, confirmation is a graduation from religious schooling, if not the Church. For still others, it's what you do because parents or grandparents would be disappointed if you didn't.

But confirmation has a much deeper and more powerful purpose than the cultural shackles we've cuffed on it in the present day. In fact, it has an intimate relationship with baptism, as intimate as the relationship between Christ and the Holy Spirit. "Amplification" and "intensification" best describe confirmation's relationship to the sacrament of baptism. This second sacrament takes what baptism gives and add "more," as the *Catechism* describes: "Confirmation perfects Baptismal grace; it is the sacrament which gives the Holy Spirit in order to root us *more deeply* in the divine filiation, incorporate us *more firmly* into Christ, strengthen our bond with the Church, associate us *more closely* with her mission, and help us bear witness to the Christian faith in words accompanied by deeds" (1316, emphasis added). Christ and, with Him, the Holy Spirit come to the Church's members in a privileged way through the sacraments. As Son and Spirit restore the divine likeness in baptism's washing, through confirmation's anointing They continue Their transformative work in us.

Another word for *anointing* is *chrismating*. For this reason, Jesus, who was anointed by the Holy Spirit at His baptism, is called "the Christ." Christians, that is, the anointed ones or *Christ*ened ones, are similarly anointed as a means to bestow the person and gifts of the Holy Spirit in greater measure. The *Jerusalem Catechesis* explains:

> When we were baptized into Christ and clothed ourselves in him, we were transformed into the likeness of the Son of God. Having destined us to be his adopted sons, God gave us a likeness to Christ in his glory, and living as we do in communion with Christ, God's anointed, we ourselves are rightly called "the anointed ones." When he said: *Do not touch my anointed ones* [or simply "christs"], God was speaking of us.... While symbolically, on our foreheads and senses, our bodies are anointed with this oil that we see, our souls are sanctified by the holy and life-giving Spirit.[218]

Returning to those days leading up to the Easter Vigil, we recall that the bishop consecrates the oil used for confirmation's anointing at the Chrism Mass. His prayer accompanied by significant gestures over the new oil—a mixture of olive oil (or another oil from plants) and fragrant balsam—has the power to deliver the divine life of the Spirit. His prayer is much like that used over the blessing of baptismal water, tracing the history of oil in the economy of salvation. The bishop recalls creation's "fruit-bearing trees," David's song of the oil of gladness, the "restoration of peace on earth with the olive branch" following the great flood, the anointing of Moses' brother, Aaron, as high priest, ending with the anointing by the Spirit upon Jesus

---

[218] *Jerusalem Catechesis*, Office of Readings for Friday within the Octave, vol. II, 608-609.

after His baptism.[219] But before the prayer begins, the bishop breathes over the opening of the vessel of Chrism. Appearing before His apostles after His Resurrection, Christ "breathed on them and said to them, 'Receive the holy Spirit'" (John 20:22). And now the bishop, standing in a superlative way in the person of Christ the High Priest, similarly sends the Holy Spirit by his breath into the Sacred Chrism, which, when used in confirmation's anointing, bestows this same mighty wind on those anointed.

The gift of the Holy Spirit finds its source not only in Christ's breath but also in the blood running from His open side. Nineteenth-century theologian and mystic Father Matthias Scheeben sees a similarity between Eve's generation from Adam's side and the "procession" or "spiration" of the Spirit from the Son. Eve and the Spirit do not find their existence through natural generation — neither is born. Rather, Eve first appears in the world from the side of the first Adam, and the Holy Spirit ushers forth eternally within the Trinity from Father and Son. But in time, when the Father's Son hangs upon the Cross, His side is pierced by the centurion's lance, His heart is opened, and out flows not only the water of baptism and the Blood of the Eucharist, but in them a "river of fire," which is the Holy Spirit.[220]

Thus, as the neophytes approach the priest to "be sealed with the gift of the Holy Spirit," the Chrism's anointing delivers the divinity of the Holy Spirit as the breath of Christ and as the spiritual river of fire from His side. By these twinned

---

[219] *The Order of the Blessing of the Oil of Catechumens and of the Sick and of Consecration of the Chrism*, no. 25.

[220] See David L. Augustine, "The Altar Fire Returns: Sacrifice and the End of Exile," in *Adoremus Bulletin* 23, no. 5 (March 2019): 6–8.

yet distinct sacraments, baptism and confirmation, the newly initiated recover the divine image lost by the Fall and subsequent sin. And now that they've been washed and perfumed, the initiates are ready for the feast. In fact, the table is already being set — literally — for the profoundest paschal experience of all: the Eucharist.

Sacrament of the Eucharist

The fourth and final element of the Easter Vigil is the celebration of the Eucharist, which the Church describes as the Vigil's "high point, for it is in the fullest sense the Easter sacrament, that is to say, the commemoration of the sacrifice of the cross and the presence of the risen Christ, the completion of Christian initiation, and the foretaste of the eternal pasch."[221] St. Albert the Great does us a great favor by connecting in memorable fashion the Vigil's Blessed Sacrament to both Holy Thursday's command to "do this" (remember?) and Good Friday's adoration of the triumphant cross. "He could not have commanded anything more beneficial," the Scholastic Doctor says, "for this sacrament is the fruit of the tree of life. Anyone who receives this sacrament with the devotion of sincere faith will never taste death. *It is a tree of life for those who grasp it, and blessed is he who holds it fast. The man who feeds on me shall live on account of me.*"[222] As St. Albert indicates, the Lord knows we hunger for Him — even if we don't always realize our hunger. With such hunger, we continue our

---

[221] *Paschalis Sollemnitatis*, no. 90.

[222] St. Albert the Great, Office of Readings for November 15 (St. Albert's feast day), vol. IV, 1560.

march toward final victory and, thankfully, all roads to heaven converge now near the end of our paschal bridge in the Eucharist.

The faithful first came to the Easter Mystery through the spectacle of the *Lucernarium*; they waxed eloquently in the poetic praise of the *Exsultet*; they proceeded to meditate on that same mystery in the Liturgy of the Word. Now, along with baptism and confirmation, there is an opportunity to experience this same mystery as a properly sacramental reality in the Liturgy of the Eucharist. In fact, in this paschal celebration, the newly baptized and confirmed participate in the Liturgy of the Eucharist for the first time in two unique ways: by helping to *offer* the sacrifice and by *receiving* that sacrifice from the altar.

To make these actions possible, we again require the indelible priestly power of Christ, the *charac*—the one that enabled the apostles to continue the memorial of Christ's sacrifice. Character, recall, conforms the recipient of the sacraments to Jesus and His three saving offices, or *munera*, the prophetic, priestly, and kingly. For this reason, the ordained priest is a sacramental manifestation of Christ the Priest. Baptism and confirmation also bestow priestly power through sacramental character, and so the Vigil's own baptized and confirmed "step into the breach," priests as they are, to offer a sacrifice that is right and just.

Their first priestly exercise, however, takes place before the Liturgy of the Eucharist, at the conclusion of the Vigil's celebration of the baptism and confirmation. As the final act of these sacraments, the priest "directs the Universal Prayer, in which the newly baptized participate for the first time."[223] Until now, following their baptism and confirmation, the previously unbaptized had been powerless to mediate—to be priests—in the

---

[223]Roman Missal, Easter Vigil, no. 58.

Universal Prayer. (As a sign of this impotency, the unbaptized candidates may have been asked to leave the assembly before this point in the Mass.) But now, as sharers in Christ's priesthood, they step forward and pray for the world in its return to God in the Universal Prayer.

Immediately following the Universal Prayer, the neophytes begin another ritual of priestly service. The Missal suggests that "the bread and wine be brought forward by the newly baptized or, if they are children, by their parents or godparents."[224] Priests offer sacrifice to God and, in so doing, reconcile giver and receiver, man with God. Without a gift to offer, the powerful priest is powerless to reconcile. But these baptismal priests offer more than simply bread and wine. Rather, they see to it that the bread and wine are true symbols of what the faithful have to offer: our prayers, works, joys, and sufferings; our love, will, and heart; our entire being. For this reason, during the Eucharistic Prayer, we will hear about the acceptable offerings of "Abel the just."[225] St. Cyprian (d. 258) explains why Abel's gift was acceptable — and why he is therefore called "the just man":

> When Cain and Abel first offered their sacrifices, God considered not so much the gifts as the spirit of the giver: God was pleased with Abel's offering because he was pleased with his spirit. Thus, Abel the just man, the peacemaker, in his blameless sacrifice taught men that when they offer their gift at the altar they should approach as he did, in the fear of God, simplicity of heart, ruled by

---

[224] Ibid., no. 60.

[225] First Eucharistic Prayer (Roman Canon), Roman Missal, Order of Mass, no. 93.

justice and peaceful harmony. Since this was the character of Abel's offering, it was only right that he himself should afterward become a sacrifice.[226]

The priest, after preparing the gifts at the altar, offers a prayer inspired by the similarly just and humble sons of Abel, the unassuming Azariah and his companions, who face incineration in the fiery furnace of the Babylonian King Nebuchadnezzar. In the midst of the flames, Azariah prays that God will receive their lives offered "with contrite heart and humble spirit" (Dan. 3:39). The priest also prays that the gifts of bread and wine may be true representations of our entire spirit, humbly and lovingly offered: "With humble spirit and contrite heart may we be accepted by you, O Lord, and may our sacrifice in your sight this day be pleasing to you, Lord God."[227] At the Easter Vigil, as at every Mass, we have priests, ordained and baptized. Each has an offering, the bread and wine filled and beating with "humble spirits and contrite hearts." St. Peter Chrysologus wonders at such priestly gifts:

> How marvelous is the priesthood of the Christian, for he is both the victim that is offered on his own behalf, and the priest who makes the offering. He does not need to go beyond himself to seek what he is to immolate to God: with himself and in himself he brings the sacrifice he is to offer God for himself. The victim remains and the priest remains, always one and the same. Immolated, the victim still lives: the priest who immolates cannot kill. Truly it

---

[226] St. Cyprian, Office of Readings for Friday of the Eleventh Week in Ordinary Time, vol. III, 377.

[227] Roman Missal, Order of Mass, no. 26.

is an amazing sacrifice in which a body is offered without being slain and blood is offered without being shed.[228]

Through such priestly power, Christ in His ordained minister transforms, perfects, and divinizes the gifts of the altar: bread and wine, men and women, which are then returned to us in the form of Holy Communion.

So far, so good—and never so excellent. But what makes this particular Eucharistic celebration different is that, in many churches on this night, souls will be offering themselves on the altar for the first time—and receiving much more in return. The Missal desires that "the newly baptized receive Holy Communion under both kinds, together with their godfathers, godmothers, and Catholic parents and spouses, as well as their lay catechists."[229] It also instructs that the faithful "receive the Lord's Body [and Blood] from the same sacrifice," that is, from the very altar upon which the sacrifice of the cross was effected.[230] After all, in their own way, the faithful have helped the priest offer this single sacrifice; they have joined their own bodies to that of Jesus, spiritually pouring their own blood into that of Jesus. As coauthors of the paschal sacrifice, it is theirs to give, and theirs to receive.

St. Gaudentius of Brescia (d. 410) sees that receiving both the Body and the Blood of Jesus in the Eucharist is a matter of weaving together bread and wine, Church and cross:

> It is appropriate that we should receive the body of Christ in the form of bread, because, as there are many grains of

---

[228] St. Peter Chrysologus, Office of Readings for Tuesday, Easter Week IV, vol. II, 771.

[229] Roman Missal, Easter Vigil, no. 65.

[230] GIRM, no. 13, citing *Sacrosanctum Concilium*, no. 55.

wheat in the flour from which bread is made by mixing it with water and baking it with fire, so also we know that many members make up the one body of Christ which is brought to maturity by the fire of the Holy Spirit.... Similarly, the wine of Christ's blood, drawn from the many grapes of the vineyard that he had planted, is extracted in the wine-press of the cross. When men receive it with believing hearts, like capacious wineskins, it ferments within them by its own power.[231]

St. Gaudentius notes that water and fire are necessary to make the bread become body. Here again, Christ and Spirit are found working together. The Holy Spirit, as we have seen, is foreshadowed not only as rain, dew, or water but also as fire. Thus, the Holy Spirit descends upon the gifts at the epiclesis, or "calling down," to moisten and bake disparate grains into a single loaf, the one Body of Christ. Besides rising like yeast within our souls, this Spirit, as St. Gaudentius suggests, also serves spirits to our souls, fermenting the new wine of grace within us. We become "filled and inebriated with the Lord himself."[232]

So that they might see clearly the truth of Christ's sacrificial Body and Blood before them, the Missal also provides an occasion for the priest, before the "Behold the Lamb of God" (*Ecce Agnus Dei*), to "briefly address the newly baptized about receiving their first Communion and about the excellence of this great mystery, which is the climax of Initiation and the center of the whole of

---

[231] St. Gaudentius of Brescia, Office of Readings for Thursday, Easter Week II, vol. II, 670.

[232] St. Leo the Great, Office of Readings for Wednesday, Easter Week II, vol. II, 661.

Christian life."[233] While presumably this same rubric did not appear in the ritual books of late fourth-century Jerusalem, the author of the *Jerusalem Catechesis* offers a model mini discourse to those about to receive the Lord in Communion for the first time — or any time:

> Since Christ himself has declared the bread to be his body, who can have any further doubt? Since he himself has said quite categorically, *This is my blood,* who would dare to question it and say that it is not his blood? Therefore, it is with complete assurance that we receive the bread and wine as the body and blood of Christ. His body is given to us under the symbol of bread, and his blood is given to us under the symbol of wine, in order to make us by receiving them one body and blood with him. Having his body and blood in our members, we become bearers of Christ and sharers, as Saint Peter says, in the divine nature.... Do not, then, regard the eucharistic elements as ordinary bread and wine: they are in fact the body and blood of the Lord, as he himself has declared. Whatever your senses may tell you, be strong in faith.[234]

Baptism, confirmation, and the high point, the Eucharist, each work together to make us "sharers in the divine nature," for each is filled with the divine nature, filled with Jesus Himself. St. Leo taught that the same Christ who fed, healed, taught, forgave, died, and rose centuries ago is the same one who feeds, heals, teaches, forgives, dies, and rises today. The difference — the only

---

[233] Roman Missal, Easter Vigil, no. 64.

[234] *Jerusalem Catechesis*, Office of Readings for Saturday within the Octave, vol. II, 621–622.

difference — is that then He did his saving deeds in the flesh, while today He does them through the sacraments.

Conclusion

We have come a long way on our paschal journey: from the dust, desert, and dung of Ash Wednesday, through the battlefield of Lent and Holy Week, up the hill of Calvary to the heights of the Cross, then down to the depths of hell, only to reemerge living and victorious before the throne of God. But the best is yet to come, and it ends where it began back in the Garden of Eden: *being like God*. And in our growth into further holiness, both neophytes and seasoned Christians are on the same footing.

Most faithful at the Easter Vigil are not there to be baptized, confirmed, or participate in the Eucharistic sacrifice for the first time. Yet the spiritual realities uncovered by the Church and her saints in this chapter are not thereby lost upon us. For these truths are ours as well, leaving and deepening their marks on us as we recall our own baptism and confirmation and relive the Eucharistic sacrifice. Despite the circumstances of our own initiation — as an infant, or outside of Easter, or with minimal ceremony — the substance of every initiate's experience is the same: Christ, His divine life, and communion with the Father and the Holy Spirit.

At the start of Lent, we heard that the forty-day season had "a double character, namely, to prepare both catechumens and faithful to celebrate the paschal mystery."[235] We have seen how the catechumens cap their paschal participation with the

---

[235] *Paschalis Sollemnitatis*, no. 6.

sacraments, while the rest of the faithful, "ever more attentive to the word of God and prayer, prepare themselves by penance for the renewal of their baptismal promises."[236] This renewal, followed by the sprinkling of the newly blessed water, takes place after the confirmation of adults (or, if there are no baptisms or initiations, following the blessing of the water). This renewal's ties to our own baptisms are obvious: holding lighted candles, we reject Satan, profess Christ, and are washed in the water from the side of Christ, the "water flowing from the Temple, from its right-hand side," as the *Vidi aquam*, the chant during the sprinkling rite, acclaims.[237]

The Easter Vigil marks the anniversary of our own initiations in a real way, both spiritually and physically. To see the Vigil's outward signs and symbols—darkness and light, paschal candle and smoke, oils and anointings, albs and candles, bread and wine—as manifestations of divine realities in our lives leads to grace, joy, happiness, and peace. It leads also to divinization, being "like God," which is the topic of our final chapter, and the final leg of the journey over Easter's paschal bridge.

In Brief

✦ Jesus, Who is the sacrament of God the Father, presents, manifests, and communicates His Paschal Mystery to us by means of the Church and her sacraments. By these sacraments, God's people cooperate in Christ's work and benefit from His victory in a most efficacious way.

---

[236] Ibid.

[237] Roman Missal, Easter Vigil, nos. 55–56.

✦ Each element of the baptismal liturgy—procession to the font, blessing of water, anointing with oil, renunciation of Satan and profession of Christ, immersion in water, vesting in white, and receiving the baptismal candle—causes the baptized to share, truly and factually, in Christ's death and Resurrection.

✦ The sacrament of confirmation amplifies and intensifies the many gifts of baptism, making us even more deeply conformed to Christ, giving us a greater share in His priestly power, and calling us to an increased responsibility in the saving life and mission of the Church. By a special outpouring of the Holy Spirit, confirmation makes us more fully alive.

✦ The newly baptized and confirmed participate in the Eucharist not only by exercising their newfound priestly power for the first time by giving to God their very selves, but also by receiving from the altar the fruits of the Cross, Christ and His Body, as food transformed and transformative.

THE NEXT TIME YOU GO TO THE EASTER VIGIL

✦ Attune your senses to the sacramental details, for what was once visible in Christ has now passed over into His sacraments (as St. Leo the Great says). God is in the details, presenting His saving power to our sensing souls in a multitude of ways.

✦ Pray for those about to be baptized, that they will, as their words profess, turn away from sin and death and toward new life in Christ. Inspired by them, and as an example to them, let your own profession—said thoughtfully and from the heart—likewise win a new lease on your life.

✦ Know that confirmation amplifies and intensifies the graces and gifts of baptism by a special outpouring of the Holy Spirit. By his breath, fire, and love, the Holy Spirit imparts God's transformative life.

✦ Offer your entire self to God during the Eucharistic Prayer: each of your prayers, works, joys, and sufferings. Get into the chalice on the altar, become a grain in the bread on the paten. God will transform these gifts of your heart, burning away the bad and inflaming the good, and He will return them, along with His Body and Blood, back to you at Communion.

9

How to Become God:
The Easter Season and Pentecost

✠

You are gods.

—John 10:34

Have you ever wondered what God will do *after* time, when creation has come and gone? Ever wondered what *we* will do after time, once we have come and gone from this earth? Wonder no longer—or at least, wonder a bit less—because the Easter season gives a glimpse of this transcendent future.

But to catch this glimpse, let's start with the wide view of time and eternity. According to St. Augustine, an awesome parallel exists between the two in the Church's paschal seasons. Earth, he says, corresponds with Lenten time, and heaven finds its earthly counterpart in Easter: "Because there are these two periods of time—the one that now is, beset with the trials and troubles of this life, and the other yet to come, a life of everlasting serenity and joy—we are given two liturgical seasons, one before Easter and the other after."[238] If the Lenten season reminds us of our

---

[238] St. Augustine, Office of Readings for Saturday, Easter Week V, vol. II, 864.

earthly origins, worldly struggles, and dusty demise, the Easter season looks ahead to our heavenly homeland and eternal reward.

These two realms may be distinct, but, thanks to Jesus' saving work, they are no longer irreparably divorced. In fact, Christ's Paschal Mystery connects earth to heaven, and Lent to Easter. Through His suffering, death, Resurrection, and Ascension, Christ builds the great bridge so that we, His people, can pass over to the opposite shore. Between Lent and Easter, we saw this bridge open before us and made present to our sacramental eyes during the Triduum: through Christ's commandments to love one another and remember His sacrificial meal on Holy Thursday, in His death upon the Cross and His opened side on Good Friday, and by His rising from the tomb on Easter morning.

Now, during the Easter season, His bridge extends not simply from Lent to Easter, but continues from earth to heaven. Our sacramental participation with the Pontifex Maximus in the liturgy becomes a living participation with Him in the world and beyond—to eternity. Our passage, in other words, only began in the baptismal font celebrated at Easter, but today, this moment—now and henceforth—continues outside the church's walls. Origen of Alexandria says, "The divine Word promises much greater and more lofty things to you who have passed through Jordan's stream by the sacrament of baptism: *he promises you a passage even through the sky.*"[239] Truly, the Paschal Mystery terminates in the interminable life of God Himself.

As a time to celebrate both here and hereafter, the Easter season gives us, the baptized and initiated, a foretaste of heaven, divinity, and divine intimacy. But Easter doesn't simply tell us

---

[239] Origen, Office of Readings for Wednesday of the Tenth Week in Ordinary Time, vol. III, 334, emphasis added.

about a distant destiny; this season participates in it, even in the present age. The Church describes these fifty days from Easter Sunday to Pentecost as "one great Sunday," an ongoing celebration of "joy and exultation."[240] It is a period when the newly initiated ("neophytes," as they are now called) receive a mystagogical catechesis that deepens their understanding of the rites celebrated at the Easter Vigil. For this reason, the Church—you and I and all the "seasoned" baptized on earth and all the saints in heaven—pray for these newborns during the Easter-season Masses, and they receive their own assigned places in the nave. Children often receive their first Holy Communion during this season, adults are encouraged to make their "Easter Duty" to receive the Eucharist,[241] and the homebound, as at the Mass of the Lord's Supper, have the Eucharist brought to them. The Church asks pastors to bless homes, visit and pray with families, and encourage expressions of popular piety.[242] As Lent sacramentalized our "campaign of Christian service" with fasting, ashes, devotions, and palms, so Easter symbolizes our "joy and exultation" in singing "Alleluia," loving one another, and praying with and for one another. In a certain sense, all of these Easter actions are a kind of fulfillment of what we were anticipating during Lent, in the same way that Christ's Resurrection is a completion of the

---

[240] *Universal Norms on the Liturgical Year and the General Roman Calendar,* no. 22.

[241] "The third precept ('You shall humbly receive your Creator in Holy Communion at least during the Easter season') guarantees as a minimum the reception of the Lord's Body and Blood in connection with the Paschal feasts, the origin and center of the Christian liturgy" (CCC 2042; see also *Code of Canon Law,* canon 920).

[242] See *Paschalis Sollemnitatis,* nos. 103–106.

Paschal Mystery that began with His Passion and death on the Cross. Now is not a time for mourning Christ's death but a time for joyfully sharing the good news of His Resurrection.

Of course, all good things must come to an end, and Easter is no exception, but before returning us to Ordinary Time, the Easter season puts an exclamation mark on its fifty days with the Solemnity of Pentecost. On this day, the faithful commemorate "the gift of the Holy Spirit to the apostles, the beginnings of the Church, and the start of its mission to all tongues and peoples and nations."[243] We know, by the way, that Pentecost is also a time of joyful celebration, because, like the beginning of Easter, Pentecost is first celebrated ideally with a Vigil not entirely unlike that of the Easter Vigil. The Vigil for Pentecost includes four readings from the Old Testament that conclude, as in the Paschal Vigil, with the Gloria and are followed by a reading from the Acts of the Apostles and the Gospel. But in place of its baptismal features, the Pentecost Vigil sacramentalizes "urgent prayer, after the example of the apostles and disciples, who persevered together in prayer with Mary, the Mother of Jesus, as they awaited the Holy Spirit."[244] In short, the Easter season, crowned by the Solemnity of Pentecost, draws the new life planted at the Easter Vigil upward to God — ascending to God, like Christ — and outward into the world. The Christ-life of the Paschal Mystery cannot be contained by mere mortals. Nor are the neophytes merely mortals; they are, if Jesus is to be believed, *gods*. Yet these are not just any gods, but human-made-divine in the image of the three-in-one, God the Father, God the Son, and God the Holy Spirit. As we will now see, each member of the Trinity brings

---

[243] Ibid., no. 107.

[244] Ibid.

His divinity to bear on our humanity, and we in turn respond to God in kind by glorifying the same Trinity in our life of faith.

Divinization by the Father

God the Father is first and foremost the Father of His beloved Son, Jesus Christ. But the Paschal Mystery also allows us to be made divine sons and daughters by the Father. The Church reminds us of this fact near the end of the Easter Season. On the Seventh Sunday of Easter, between the Lord's Ascension, forty days after His Resurrection, and the Holy Spirit's descent, fifty days after Christ's rising, the Church reads from the "High-Priestly Prayer" of Jesus.[245] These words, spoken to His apostles at the Last Supper, were also recommended for our meditation during the short period of adoration that followed the Mass of the Lord's Supper on Holy Thursday. In this remarkable text, Jesus discloses the nature of the intimacy between God and man that His priestly mediation brings about. These two reconciled parties, the divine and human, enjoy more than the simple peace and harmony that characterized their relationship before the Fall, when God walked and talked with Adam and Eve in the garden. Now, after Jesus' redeeming work, the relationship between God and man, heaven and earth, is one of sharing in God's divine life. The Devil was right about one thing: we were to be like gods, but not because of his diabolical say-so, nor because of man's prideful willing so. Rather, it was due to God's divine *doing so* — His becoming man and rising from the tomb — that we can now share in His divinity. Jesus prays to the Father at the Last Supper:

---

[245] Where the Ascension of the Lord has been transferred from Thursday of the sixth Week of Easter to the seventh Week of Easter, the readings proper to the Ascension are used and those from John 17 are supplanted.

I pray not only for them, but also for those who will be-lieve in me through their word, so that they may all be one, as you, Father, are in me and I in you, that they also may be in us, that the world may believe that you sent me. And I have given them the glory you gave me, so that they may be one, as we are one, I in them and you in me, that they may be brought to perfection as one, that the world may know that you sent me, and that you loved them even as you loved me. (John 17:20–23)

Even da Vinci's *Last Supper* could not depict so divine an inti-macy: "I have given them the glory you gave me, so that they may be one, as we are one, I in them and you in me, that they may be brought to perfection." This intimate sharing in the divine nature is called "divinization," or *theosis*. It is a transformative closeness that elevates and perfects our human nature to a degree unimaginable by the world before Christ's advent.

But this mysterious transformation should be no mystery to anyone who understands how we first gained life in Christ. Divi-nization begins with baptism. The Second Sunday of Easter, known commonly as "Divine Mercy Sunday," is today less commonly known by its more traditional name, "Quasimodo Sunday." The name comes not from Quasimodo, Victor Hugo's hunchbacked bell ringer of Notre Dame; strictly speaking, it comes from the opening words of the entrance antiphon, or Introit, for that day: *Quasimodo geniti infantes*—"Like newborn infants, you must long for the pure, spiritual milk, that in him you may grow to salvation, alleluia."[246] Our birth from the font, while similar to our natural

---

[246] But Victor Hugo's Quasimodo is very much related to this celebration, as the character took his name from the Second Sunday of Easter, the day he was found by the cathedral's archdeacon on Notre Dame's steps.

birth from our human mother, places us in a higher realm, a supernatural world, where life pulses not simply with human blood but with divine grace, the lifeblood of a new existence. "On this day is created the true man," writes St. Gregory of Nyssa (d. 394), "the man made in the image and likeness of God. For *this day the Lord has made* is the beginning of this new world."[247] This "newborn infant" or new, "true man" is as human as any other. But his humanity partakes also in God's divinity. While not God as Jesus is God, the baptized nevertheless exude (to the degree their finite nature allows) both humanity *and* divinity.

The irony, of course, is that, as we noted above, "being like God" was a part of that mix making a mess of mankind in the first place! Recall, Adam and Eve had been created from the beginning "like God." But wanting to be even *more* like God—which we all should, as this is life's purpose—they misguidedly grasped (with some help from the Enemy) at divinity on their own. As we heard St. Maximus the Confessor (d. 662) explain, they wished to be like God but "without God, before God, and not in accordance with God."[248] Our circuitous route to divinity was thus beset with hardship, suffering, death, and hell. Now, after the Easter Resurrection, we are once again face-to-face with God—even heart to heart—His divinity before us. It's not exactly "within our grasp"—let's not make that mistake again!—but it is offered to us in abundance as our eternal patrimony and ultimate destiny.

The Church Fathers spoke regularly and emphatically about this divine destiny. Following the Fall, the Lord stationed "the cherubim and the fiery revolving sword east of the garden of Eden,

---

[247] St. Gregory of Nyssa, Office of Readings for Monday, Easter Week V, vol. II, 826.

[248] St. Maximus the Confessor, as quoted in CCC 398.

to guard the way to the tree of life" (Gen. 3:24). But now, after baptism, the Church tells us that these same cherubim serve a different role. The ancient homily we read at Holy Saturday's Office of Readings (see pages 108–110) hears Jesus saying to Adam upon his imminent return from hell, "I appointed cherubim to guard you as slaves are guarded, but *now I make them worship you as God.* The throne formed by cherubim awaits you, its bearers swift and eager."[249] Adam to Adam, man to mankind, Jesus has done a great work in hell and come back to tell us about it, reversing the course of human nature forever. Arrogantly grasping at divinity, our parents are evicted from paradise, the cherubim guarding them with flaming sword. Jesus' blood, as St. Leo the Great says, extinguishes the fiery sword,[250] and now these same cherubim form our very throne at God's right hand. Has history ever seen such a turn of events?

Such a great gift man has been given! The *Catechism* invokes St. Athanasius's brief though profound maxim concerning our divinization: "For the Son of God became man *so that we might become God*" (CCC 460, emphasis added). But Christ's incarnate work for our transformation into divinization was just the beginning: today, in the Age of the Church, He continues His work in us through the sacraments. St. Cyril of Alexandria explains, "After Christ had completed his mission on earth, it still remained necessary for us to become *sharers in the divine nature of the Word.* We had to give up our own life and be so transformed that we would begin to live an entirely new kind of life that would be

---

[249] Ancient homily, Office of Readings for Holy Saturday, vol. II, 497–498, emphasis added.

[250] St. Leo the Great, Office of Readings for Thursday, Lent Week IV, vol. II, 313.

pleasing to God."[251] And in perhaps the clearest expression of this *theosis*, this sharing in the divine nature, St. Basil the Great (d. 379) announces, "Through the Spirit we acquire a likeness to God; indeed, we attain what is beyond our most sublime aspirations—*we become God*."[252]

So far, we have been looking to the Eastern Fathers for our understanding of this great work of mankind sharing in God's divinity. But the Western Doctors affirm the same truth about divinization. In a sermon on the Ascension of Jesus, Pope St. Leo the Great sees the time between Christ's Resurrection and Ascension as a period emphasizing our wonderful transformation: "Beloved, the days which passed between the Lord's resurrection and his ascension were by no means uneventful; during them, great sacramental mysteries were confirmed, great truths revealed." Citing the example of the disciples on the road to Emmaus, Pope Leo writes:

> Their eyes were opened in the breaking of bread, opened far more happily to *the sight of their own glorified humanity* than were the eyes of our first parents to the shame of their sin.... Indeed, that blessed company [of apostles] had a great and inexpressible cause for joy when it saw man's nature rising above the dignity of the whole heavenly creation, above the ranks of angels, above the exalted status of archangels. *Nor would there be any limit to its upward course* until humanity was admitted to a seat at

---

[251] St. Cyril of Alexandria, Office of Readings for Thursday, Easter Week VII, vol. II, 990, emphasis added.

[252] St. Basil the Great, Office of Readings for Tuesday, Easter Week VII, vol. II, 976, emphasis added.

the right hand of the eternal Father, to be enthroned at last in the glory of him to whose nature it was wedded in the person of the Son.[253]

Centuries later, the Angelic Doctor, St. Thomas Aquinas, intoned this same lofty theme: "Since it was the will of God's only-begotten Son that men should share in his divinity, he assumed our nature in order that by becoming man *he might make men gods.*"[254] The Church, in her accumulated and grace-filled wisdom, thus sees a glorified greatness in our future (and in our present, as we shall see in our concluding chapter). But what about us? Do we see that the saving work Christ accomplished for us is no mere Band-Aid to hide our wounded sinfulness or disguise to mask our fallen faces? By the light of the paschal candle, first lit at the Easter Vigil, we have our answer: our sinful selves appear more beautiful, living fuller lives than Adam and Eve ever could have. We were made for greatness, and the Easter season does its liturgical and sacramental best to bring our divine potential to actual fact.

In the beginning, Father, Son, and Holy Spirit cooperated in our creation from dust. Irenaeus of Lyon (d. 202) likened the Trinity to a Father with two creative hands—one hand, His Son, and the other, the Holy Spirit. Today, at our new beginning, God the Father works His new creation with the same Son and Holy Spirit, by these hands forming men and women in His divine likeness. All three Divine Persons cooperate in all their

---

[253] St. Leo the Great, Office of Readings for Wednesday, Easter Week VI, vol. II, 898–899, emphasis added.

[254] St. Thomas Aquinas, Office of Readings for the Feast of Corpus Christi, vol. III, 610, emphasis added.

actions of creation and governance. We already have seen how, for example, Son and Holy Spirit led us into the promised land of the church at the Easter Vigil. These same hands re-form those of us who are de-formed into living reflections of the Father's face during this season. The Easter season is time to grow the divine life implanted in us at the Paschal Triduum, and it does so through the Son and the Holy Spirit working in time—and overtime—through the sacraments.

Divinization through the Son

If we are sons and daughters of God the Father, it naturally follows that we are also made brothers and sisters of God the Son, Jesus Christ. To accomplish this heavenly adoption, the dynamics of our divinization in the post-resurrection world are sacramental. Created by God, we naturally bear the supernatural image. At the Incarnation of Jesus, when Mary said, "Yes!," our shared intimacy deepened. Now, by membership in His Church after receiving Him in the initiation sacraments, our participation in the divine nature reaches its zenith. Reflecting on Jesus' high-priestly prayer, the twelfth-century Cistercian Blessed Isaac of Stella preached:

> Therefore, the whole body with its head is Son of Man, Son of God, and God. This is the explanation of the Lord's words: *Father, I desire that as you and I are one, so they may be one with us.* . . . When all are united with God they become one God. The Son of God is one with God by nature; the Son of Man is one with him in his person; we, his body, are one with him sacramentally. Consequently, those who by faith are spiritual members

of Christ can truly say that they are what he is: the Son
of God *and God himself.*[255]

Here is the key to understanding our divinization in Christ, Isaac
seems to say: our union with God must be sacramental. Indeed,
to be a cell of Christ's Mystical Body means, as a consequence,
to be infused with the very lifeblood of that simultaneously divine and human organism. The Church, we've already noted,
is the great sacrament by which we are all literally incorporated
into the life of Christ; likewise, the seven sacraments serve as
particular and powerful means to achieving that incorporation,
and then thriving within the Church and the world.

In baptism, for example, we gain entrance into this "wondrous
sacrament of the whole Church."[256] For this reason, the Church
describes baptism as a "gateway," "door," and point of "access"
(CCC 1213). Likewise, our membership in the Mystical Body
is amplified and intensified by the sacrament of confirmation
and nourished and grows by means of the sacrament of the Eucharist. St. Hilary of Poitiers (d. 368), commenting as well on
Jesus' words at the Last Supper (John 14:19–20), describes the
process this way:

> The manner of our indwelling in him through the sacra-
> ment of his body and blood is evident from the Lord's
> own words: *This world will see me no longer but you shall see
> me. Because I live you shall live also, for I am in my Father,
> you are in me, and I am in you.* If it had been a question
> of a mere unity of will, why should he have given us this

---

[255] Blessed Isaac of Stella, Office of Readings for Friday, Easter Week V, vol.
II, 856, emphasis added.

[256] *Sacrosanctum Concilium*, no. 5.

explanation of the steps by which it is achieved? He is in the Father by reason of his divine nature, we are in him by reason of his human birth, and *he is in us through the mystery of the sacraments.*[257]

Christ even integrates mankind's physical nature into the salvific work of the Church. The Mystical Body parallels the natural body in its generation, nurturing, and growth; thus, participation in the divine nature within the sacrament of the Church begins, strengthens, and increases by the sacraments of the Church.

Nor is this sacramental incorporation lost on St. Augustine in his writings on the divinizing power of the Eucharist. St. Augustine imagines Jesus telling him from the Host, "I am the food of grown men; grow, and you shall feed upon me; nor shall you change me, like the food of your flesh, into yourself, but you shall be changed into me."[258] Unlike the terrestrial fare we eat to maintain life and mobility, when we consume the Eucharistic Body, it consumes us — digesting and transforming the baptized into the Son of God.

The food that Christ offers to us is indeed eternal, and the drink He offers is everlasting life, as St. Leo the Great notes, tasting the same divinization in Jesus' Precious Blood that St. Augustine found in the Blessed Host. When we, baptized, new creatures that we are, receive Holy Communion, St. Leo writes, we are "filled and inebriated with the Lord himself. For the effect of our sharing in the body and blood of Christ is to change

---

[257] St. Hilary, Office of Readings for Wednesday, Easter Week IV, vol. II, 779, emphasis added.

[258] Quoted in Pope Benedict XVI, Post-Synodal Apostolic Exhortation *Sacramentum Caritatis* (February 22, 2007), no. 70.

us into what we receive."[259] "Eat, drink, and make merry," St. Augustine and St. Leo seem to say, "for today we live in Christ!" In fact, Holy Communion will lead us to a "sober drunkenness."[260] Such a potent brew of clarity and joy is possible only through the Son, who is Logos, providing sobriety, logic, and reason, and the Holy Spirit, whose "spirited" joyfulness goes straight to our heads (and hearts!), offering us a divinely intoxicating release from the grave and mundane matters of earthly life.

The sacraments may have the final word on divinization, but they aren't the only word. In fact, the Holy Word of God also transforms the members of Jesus' Mystical Body into divine echoes of the eternal Logos. In few words, St. Gregory the Great (d. 604) explains this truth to his flock, noting, "The divine words grow together with the one who reads them."[261] The Word, received by the ear, enters our hearts, and from this core of our being it circulates through our bodies, transforming the deeds of our hands, the step of our feet, and the words of our mouths. The "growing together" leads us to "sound like" the Logos we hear. Pope Benedict XVI named the transformative process as the "logicizing" of our being:[262] we get "Worded" by and in the Word.

Christ is present in the sacraments, and especially so in the Blessed Sacrament; but He is also present in each scriptural word in the liturgy, a fact that we cannot forget if we are to speak with the power of divinity and "sound like" that which we speak. Recalling the epic nature of the Easter Vigil's Liturgy

---

[259] St. Leo the Great, Office of Readings for Wednesday, Easter Week II, vol. II, 661.

[260] See Guardini, *The Spirit of the Liturgy*, 27.

[261] Quoted in Pope Benedict XVI, *Verbum Domini*, no. 30.

[262] Ratzinger, *The Spirit of the Liturgy*, 58.

of the Word — eight readings, a slew of psalms, and the Gospel! — this means of eternal transformation, divinization, and *theosis* in Christ is given us in abundance during the Easter season. By hearing the inspired Word and receiving worthily His sacraments, we find our rightful place in the Mystical Body and thrive as members of that same body.

Divinization in the Holy Spirit

Christ, working in His Body and His sacraments, also continues to act with the Holy Spirit. He has never lived or worked alone, but always with the Holy Spirit unto the glory of the Father. So, too, in this Age of the Church does the Holy Spirit animate our participation in God's life and likeness.

At the Easter Vigil, we witnessed the paschal candle immersed in the baptismal font. One interpretation of the action, and one informed by the texts prayed at that moment, sees the Holy Spirit descending upon the font as an *epiclesis*, a coming down. There is, then, a resemblance between the Holy Spirit overshadowing the Blessed Mother at Christ's conception in her womb. So, too, the same Spirit descends during the Easter Vigil upon the womb of the Church, the font, giving birth to Christians. As we saw, the fourth-century Church Father Didymus of Alexandria goes so far as to call the Holy Spirit our *parent*. As noted earlier, Didymus writes, "We men are conceived twice: to the human body we owe our first conception, to the divine Spirit, our second." We rise, he adds, from earthly ashes to heavenly grace:

> Finding us in a state of deformity, the Spirit restores our
> original beauty and fills us with his grace, leaving no

room for anything unworthy of our love. The Spirit frees us from sin and death, and changes us from the earthly men we were, men of dust and ashes, into spiritual men, sharers in the divine glory, sons and heirs of God the Father who bear a likeness to the Son and are his co-heirs and brothers, destined to reign with him and to share his glory. In place of earth the Spirit reopens heaven to us and gladly admits us into paradise, giving us even now greater honor than the angels, and by the holy waters of baptism extinguishing the unquenchable fires of hell.[263]

The association between the water, as found in baptism, and the Holy Spirit is foreshadowed throughout the Old Covenant, as we heard recounted in the prayer of Blessing over the Font. The Holy Spirit hovered over the waters of creation, regenerated human life after Noah's flood, conquered Pharaoh and his army with water, anointed Christ emerging from the waters of the Jordan, and came forth as water from Christ's side. This same living water — recall that St. Cyril of Jerusalem calls it "leaping water"[264] — transforms and divinizes Christians today, refreshing them from first lap to final stretch in their race to heaven.

The Holy Spirit also continues His outpouring upon us today. His outpouring is a beautifully unitive principle in the Mystical Body and at the same time a unique response to the requirements of each soul — both those newly transformed at baptism and those in need of constant rejuvenation. Accordingly, while

---

[263] Didymus of Alexandria, Office of Readings for Monday, Easter Week VI, vol. II, 882–883.

[264] St. Cyril of Jerusalem, Office of Readings for Monday, Easter Week VII, vol. II, 967.

generally we all follow a common bridge to sanctity, each does so by a uniquely unrepeatable path. The Holy Spirit, acting upon each individual cell in the one Body of Christ, descends "like the rain," says St. Cyril of Jerusalem. Why rain? "Always the same in itself," he writes, water "produces many different effects, one in the palm tree, another in the vine, and so on throughout the whole of creation." Similarly, in the customized process of *theosis*, St. Cyril adds:

> The Spirit makes one man a teacher of divine truth, inspires another to prophesy, gives another the power of casting out devils, enables another to interpret holy Scripture. The Spirit strengthens one man's self-control, shows another how to help the poor, teaches another to fast and lead a life of asceticism, makes another oblivious to the needs of the body, trains another for martyrdom. His action is different in different people, but the Spirit himself is always the same. *In each person,* Scripture says, *the Spirit reveals his presence in a particular way for the common good.*[265]

The Chosen People sang of the many roads that lead to the Temple, the dwelling place of God and their hoped-for destination. "As they go through the Baca Valley," Psalm 84 says, for example, "they make it a place of springs; the autumn rain covers it with pools" (verse 7, Revised Grail Psalms). The Chosen People's song is now ours. But whereas they sang of shadows, we sing in the full light of Christ about the Holy Spirit, who waters our path to heaven and restores the garden of God and man.

Christ life is the grace that transforms us, not only through baptism but also through confirmation and the Eucharist (and,

---

[265] Ibid.

of course, via every sacrament). So, too, the Holy Spirit has the power to transform. When reflecting upon the sacrament of confirmation during the Easter Vigil, we witnessed how the side of the Second Adam was pierced and a "river of fire" flowed out, igniting the lives of the baptized and fanning into flame the newly inspired faith. But God is ever renewing His promise to us, and so, naturally (that is, supernaturally), the Solemnity of Pentecost, which concludes the Easter Season, marks a second special outpouring of the "river of fire" upon the Church.

This same variety within unity was also present at the Church's creation. At history's new Pentecost, the Holy Spirit inspired each of the apostles to speak in different tongues and proclaim the good news to all the disparate and devout Jews in Jerusalem. Despite the difference in language among the city's visitors—some were Parthians, Medes, and Elamites, to name a few—each group heard the apostles in its own tongue. The account is read each year at Mass for Pentecost (Acts 2:1–11). The story ends with the suggestion of some suspicious witnesses wondering if the apostles had too much to drink: "But others said, scoffing, 'They have had too much new wine'" (verse 13). "Spirits" is a secular term for strong alcohol, but it is neverthe-less related to the Holy Spirit. An anonymous sixth-century sermon offers support for the "spirited" theory of drunkenness: "some people were not far wrong in saying: *They have been drink-ing too much new wine*. The truth is that the disciples had now become fresh wineskins, renewed and made holy by grace. The new wine of the Holy Spirit filled them, so that their fervor brimmed over and they spoke in manifold tongues."[266] Thus,

---

[266] Sermon by a sixth-century African author, Office of Readings from Saturday, Easter Week VII, vol. II, 1006.

not only does the Holy Spirit bestow His divinizing power upon those overshadowed at Pentecost and confirmation, but the Eucharist also conveys the transformative power of the Spirit to worthy recipients.

The Eucharist becomes not only the living God dwelling among us but also the epicenter for the Holy Spirit's *epiclesis*. In the Second Eucharistic Prayer, the priest asks God to sanctify our offerings "by sending down your Spirit upon them like the dewfall."[267] In this *epiclesis*, the life-giving moisture of the Holy Spirit works a transformative effect. The "dew" of the Spirit first appeared to the Chosen People as they crossed the desert on their way to the promised land. Tired of the food God was serving them, the Lord not only gave them quail in the evening, but in the morning the Chosen People also found "a layer of dew all about the camp, and when the layer of dew evaporated, fine flakes were on the surface of the wilderness, fine flakes like hoarfrost on the ground" (Exod. 16:13–14). As the new Chosen People, we Catholics, too, are complaining pilgrims on our passage to the Promised Land, and God, in turn, gives us a new manna, sending His Spirit "like the dewfall" upon our offerings, represented by the Mass's bread. But unlike our ancestors who died, "whoever eats this bread will live forever" (John 6:58).

The spiritual dew that moistens our sacrificial bread at the altar also gives new life to us who offer and receive it. The Body of Christ that is the Church draws its life from the Body of Christ that is the Eucharist.[268] And as the many grains of wheat come

---

[267] Roman Missal, Order of Mass, 101.

[268] See Pope John Paul II, Encyclical Letter *Ecclesia de Eucharistia* (April 17, 2003).

together in one sacrificial host, so the many cells of the Mystical Body, watered and baked by the same Holy Spirit, unite in a single *Corpus Christi*. As St. Irenaeus explains, "This was why the Lord had promised to send the Advocate: he was to prepare us as an offering to God. Like dry flour, which cannot become one lump of dough, one loaf of bread, without moisture, we who are many could not become one in Christ Jesus without the water that comes down from heaven."[269] As our accuser, the Devil, was cast down to hell like lightning, St. Irenaeus continues, we need the "dew of God" to be cast down upon us, lest we be made "scorched and unfruitful."[270]

This entire chapter has sought to demonstrate that mankind is truly destined for great things if it puts its faith, hope, and love in Christ. Indeed, *theosis* delivers a one-two punch from God the Father's re-creative hands: with the first blow, we receive the Son, and with the second, we receive the Spirit, both infusing our souls with divine power. Divine life has been the entire purpose of Lent, the Triduum, and the Easter Season. We stand ready now to conclude our Easter journey, and we look back at the path we've traveled for nearly a hundred days, beginning in dust and ash. Since that first smudged mark of the cross on an otherwise ordinary Wednesday, we have been watered from Christ's side at Easter and inspired by His Spirit at Pentecost — and now have become men and women fully alive. We have found in the Easter Mystery what the world has been searching for. In a sense, we have become that mystery, in body, soul, humanity — and divinity.

---

[269] St. Irenaeus, Office of Readings for Pentecost, vol. II, 1025.

[270] Ibid., 1026.

Conclusion

Pentecost concludes the Easter Season, but it does not complete our journey through the Easter Mystery. We began with dirty foreheads, battled to win Calvary's grubby hill by prayer, fasting, and love of neighbor, and found ourselves at last at the first fire of Easter. Christ's sacraments destroyed the Devil, and His Cross provided the material for our paschal bridge to heaven. Led by a Pillar of Fire and a Column of Cloud, accompanied by a host of angels and marching with a band of saints, we grappled with the Devil and emerged victorious. We can truly see supernatural life within our sights, there on the other side of death, and through this same supernatural life we are given a fresh start to live the life of God. May Father, Son, and Spirit protect us—even from ourselves—and never let the divine image leave our radiant faces! The Church's Pentecost prayer is a fitting watchword now and forever:

> Grant, we pray, almighty God,
> that the splendor of your glory
> may shine forth upon us
> and that, by the bright rays of the Holy Spirit,
> the light of your light may confirm the hearts
> of those born again by your grace.
> Through our Lord Jesus Christ, your Son,
> who lives and reigns with you in the unity of
>   the Holy Spirit,
> one God, for ever and ever.
> Amen.[271]

Thanks be to God, alleluia, alleluia!

---

[271] Roman Missal, Collect for the Pentecost Vigil (Simple Form), second option.

In Brief

✦ The Easter Season, concluding with Pentecost, continues our paschal journey: not only does it receive us after our passing over from Lent, but it launches our crossing from the mundane world to the divine Promised Land.

✦ God, our Father and Creator, made us in His image and likeness. But despite our best efforts to resist His great gift of divine life, He allows its restoration by the paschal work of Jesus and the reanimating efforts of the Holy Spirit. The Father sends His Son, and by the Son's gift of the Spirit, "we acquire a likeness to God; indeed, we attain what is beyond our most sublime aspirations — we become God" (St. Basil the Great).

✦ Jesus effects our divinization — our divine adoption as His brothers and sisters — through the sacraments and the revealed Word of God. By receiving them, *Christ receives us*, transforming us into His divine likeness.

✦ The Holy Spirit, constant cooperator with the Son for the Father's glory, works with Jesus in the sacraments to animate our new, divine life. The Holy Spirit amplifies and clarifies His divinizing presence at Pentecost, the final feast of Easter's fifty-day season.

THE NEXT TIME YOU CELEBRATE
THE EASTER SEASON

✦ See the journey home to its completion. You were made for greatness: you were made to share in God's life.

✦ Salvation doesn't happen by our will alone, nor does it happen against our will. Rather, living the divine life of grace is a cooperation between you and God. God will shower His gifts abundantly during the Easter season, so be sure to offer Him prayer, sacrifices, and actions that He can perfect and complete.

✦ Pray a novena to the Holy Spirit (many versions exist) in the days leading up to Pentecost: *O Father, who taught the hearts of the faithful by the light of the Holy Spirit, grant that, by this same Spirit, I may be truly wise and ever rejoice in His consolation. Through the same Christ our Lord. Amen.*

CONCLUSION

In the Land of the Living

✠

There is something extraordinary about their lives.
—From the Epistle to Diognetus[272]

The Paschal Mystery is not easily contained in the liturgies, sacraments, and devotions of the Lent and Easter seasons—it's much too large for these finite expressions. It's as if human expression were a tabernacle, seeking to contain the infinite and eternal in the finite and temporal. For this reason, the Church presents Christ's saving work in a myriad of ways: sacramental signs such as ashes, palms, and candles; Sacred Scripture to a degree not heard throughout the rest of the year; music and poetry (which have their own sort of language) such as Holy Thursday's *Ubi caritas* and the Easter Vigil's *Exsultet*. These smaller threads combine to portray to our senses the tapestry of the Easter Mystery. Even the analogies employed throughout the tradition and in this book, while true, remain limited. This devotional journey into the Easter Mystery we have taken resembles at times an exodus from slavery to freedom, at other

---

[272] From a letter to Diognetus, Office of Readings for Wednesday, Easter Week V, 840.

times a pilgrimage to our heavenly home, and at still other times a procession from death to life. It is also likened, rightly, to building a bridge from earth to heaven. Or, as the Church suggested at Lent's outset, climbing "the Holy mountain of Easter."[273] It's from this last image — the Holy mountain — that we'll descend in this concluding chapter.

We have seen how a close look at the rites and texts of Lent and Easter reveal a great treasure: Christ. But how can we spend this treasure, as it were, in the world, in the day-to-day lives each of us is called to live?

The figure of Moses has been a helpful guide throughout our journey, just as he was for the Chosen People as they passed out of Egypt into the relative freedom east of the Red Sea. He now models for us a proper descent from a mountainous encounter with God back to earth. Following their exodus from Egypt, the holy people arrived at Mount Sinai, where God revealed His laws to the people and formed a covenant with them. Moses was the great mediator between God and the people: he spoke to the people on behalf of God, and he spoke to God on behalf of the people. Indeed, man though Moses was, "The LORD used to speak to Moses face to face, as a person speaks to a friend" (Exod. 33:11). But such intimate conversing with God had a transformative effect on Moses. More than merely the messenger of God, Moses began to resemble the Lord: the divine presence rubbed off on him and left its mark. The book of Exodus recounts Moses' forty days and nights on the mountain, and if this number reminds you of Lent's forty days and nights, it should. While visiting with God on the mountaintop, Moses transcribed the Lord's words of the covenant.

---

[273] *Paschalis Sollemnitatis*, no. 6.

But then, "As Moses came down from Mount Sinai with the two tablets of the covenant in his hands, he did not know that the skin of his face had become radiant while he spoke with the LORD. When Aaron, then, and the other Israelites saw Moses and noticed how radiant the skin of his face had become, they were afraid to come near him" (Exod. 34:29–30). The Israelites were suddenly struck with a great "fear of the Lord" because they recognized who God the Almighty was, and how lowly they were in comparison. It is for this reason that they first sent Moses to the mountain to speak to God on their behalf. "Do not let God speak to us," they implored him, "or we shall die" (Exod. 20:19). And here was that same divine power and glory returning with Moses into their camps! To lessen their fear, Moses had to "put a veil over his face" when he spoke to the people, thus dimming the Lord's radiance and hiding his power; only when returning to speak to the Lord atop the mountain would he lift the veil again (Exod. 34:33–35).

A similarly transformative event happens for Jesus and the apostles Peter, James, and John atop Mount Tabor, which we heard about at Mass on the Second Sunday of Lent. In the account, Moses and Elijah appear with Jesus and discuss "his exodus that he was going to accomplish in Jerusalem" (Luke 9:31). He is then transfigured before the apostles' eyes, "and his clothes became dazzling white, such as no fuller on earth could bleach them" (Mark 9:3). Quite the spectacle for Peter, James, and John: they went from being drowsy with sleep to "becoming fully awake" (Luke 9:32), and then "terrified" (Mark 9:6), much as the Israelites had upon catching sight of the luminous Moses. In fact, as Jesus and the disciples come down from the mountain and back to the ordinary world, the large crowd that first sees him is "utterly amazed" (Mark 9:14–15). Here again, meeting God atop His holy mountain transforms those within His aura.

Do these two episodes have any bearing on us during this post-Easter period? Indeed, they do!

Moses passed over from death to life as a type or foreshadow. Jesus passed over from death to life in fulfillment of that shadow —that is, in supernatural reality. By the Church's sacraments and sacramental liturgy, those responding to the Lord's call truly pass over to heaven. The same pattern also emerges in our own transfiguration. Moses encountered the Lord atop Mount Sinai, was himself changed, and he carried the divine presence back into the world. Jesus was transformed on Mount Tabor, was transfigured, and returned in His amazing radiance back into the fallen world. You and I have climbed Easter's holy mountain along our devotional journey, have been changed by its radiance — divinized, as we said in the last chapter — and now, with the joy and fervor of Easter on our lips and in our hearts, it is time to reenter the world and radiate God's glory in its darkened corners. For the new life of grace lived by Christ's new men and women isn't meant simply for ourselves, nor is it confined to the church's walls. Neither is the promise of divinization to wait until after death. On the contrary, grace-filled Christians usher in a new heaven and a new earth *today*.

Between our supernatural baptism and our natural death, a great deal of working and living needs to happen. Even though we all emerge from a church's baptismal font as Catholics and, God willing, we return to its cemetery soil as Catholics, for most of us, life happens in the world and not in or around a church building. The liturgy, the Second Vatican Council says, is the source and summit of the Church's activity.[274] We Catholics who live in the world must see this same source and summit as our

---

[274] *Sacrosanctum Concilium*, nos. 10, 14.

inheritance as well. Its refulgent[275] celebrations impel us — like an eruption — into the world and onto its streets to transform them. God transforms the natural matter of the sacraments, such as the Eucharist; the sacraments divinize the faithful; and the faithful sanctify the world.

Holiness, then, is not reserved for the afterlife but needs living today. In fact, "the living" was another name for the early Christians, those who in spirit, soul, and body understood the great gift given them by God. Pope Benedict XVI explains the vibrance of today's divine life this way:

> "Eternal life" is not — as the modern reader might immediately assume — life after death, in contrast to this present life, which is transient and not eternal. "Eternal life" is life itself, real life, which can also be lived in the present age and is no longer challenged by physical death. This is the point: to seize "life" here and now, real life that can no longer be destroyed by anything or anyone.... A distinguishing feature of the disciple of Jesus is that he "lives": beyond the mere fact of existing, he has found and embraced the *real* life that everyone is seeking. On the basis of such texts, the early Christians called themselves simply "the living" (*hoi zōntes*). They had found what all are seeking — life itself, full and, hence, indestructible life.[276]

---

[275] The Church's liturgical rites, the Fathers of the Second Vatican Council say, are to "radiate noble simplicity" (*ritus nobili simplicitate fulgeant*, "let the rites shine with noble simplicity"). *Sacrosanctum Concilium*, no. 34.

[276] Pope Benedict XVI, *Jesus of Nazareth: Holy Week* (San Francisco: Ignatius Press, 2011), 82–83.

Pope Benedict describes precisely what Jesus means when He announces that He "came so that they might have life and have it more abundantly" (John 10:10).

Eternal life—indestructible, joyful, abundant—not only proves transformative for those possessing it, but it also animates the world we inhabit. In her Office of Readings during the Fifth week of Easter, the Church describes to "the living" how to live in the world, what to expect from the world in return, and their obligation to witness to Life itself. Because this point is essential to understanding the project of this book—how to journey into the Easter Mystery and beyond—it is worth quoting at length from the Epistle to Diognetus,[277] an anonymous letter written in the second century and one of the earliest examples of Christian apologetics:

> Christians are indistinguishable from other men either by nationality, language or customs. They do not inhabit separate cities of their own, or speak a strange dialect, or follow some outlandish way of life. Their teaching is not based upon reveries inspired by the curiosity of men. Unlike some other people, they champion no purely human doctrine. With regard to dress, food and manner of life in general, they follow the customs of whatever city they happen to be living in, whether it is Greek or foreign.
>
> And yet there is something extraordinary about their lives. They live in their own countries as though they were only passing through. They play their full role as

---

[277] A certain Diognetus served as tutor to the second-century Roman emperor and philosopher Marcus Aurelius, but many scholars doubt that this is the same individual. Otherwise, the recipient of this famous letter is unknown.

citizens, but labor under all the disabilities of aliens. Any country can be their homeland, but for them their homeland, wherever it may be, is a foreign country. Like others, they marry and have children, but they do not expose them. They share their meals, but not their wives. They live in the flesh, but they are not governed by the desires of the flesh. They pass their days upon earth, but they are citizens of heaven. Obedient to the laws, they yet live on a level that transcends the law.

Christians love all men, but all men persecute them. Condemned because they are not understood, they are put to death, but raised to life again. They live in poverty, but enrich many; they are totally destitute, but possess an abundance of everything. They suffer dishonor, but that is their glory. They are defamed, but vindicated. A blessing is their answer to abuse, deference their response to insult. For the good they do they receive the punishment of malefactors, but even then they rejoice, as though receiving the gift of life. They are attacked by the Jews as aliens, they are persecuted by the Greeks, yet no one can explain the reason for this hatred.

To speak in general terms, we may say that the Christian is to the world what the soul is to the body. As the soul is present in every part of the body, while remaining distinct from it, so Christians are found in all the cities of the world, but cannot be identified with the world. As the visible body contains the invisible soul, so Christians are seen living in the world, but their religious life remains unseen. The body hates the soul and wars against it, not because of any injury the soul has done it, but because of the restriction the soul places on its pleasures. Similarly, the world hates the Christians, not because they have done it any wrong, but because they are opposed to its enjoyments.

Christians love those who hate them just as the soul loves the body and all its members despite the body's hatred. It is by the soul, enclosed within the body, that the body is held together, and similarly, it is by the Christians, detained in the world as in a prison, that the world is held together. The soul, though immortal, has a mortal dwelling place; and Christians also live for a time amidst perishable things, while awaiting the freedom from change and decay that will be theirs in heaven. As the soul benefits from the deprivation of food and drink, so Christians flourish under persecution. Such is the Christian's lofty and divinely appointed function, from which he is not permitted to excuse himself.[278]

One is reminded in this letter of St. Paul's observation that, in preaching the gospel, Christians truly do not fit into the world as we know it. "For Jews demand signs and Greeks look for wisdom, but we proclaim Christ crucified, a stumbling block to Jews and foolishness to Gentiles, but to those who are called, Jews and Greeks alike, Christ the power of God and the wisdom of God" (1 Cor. 1:22–24). So we all are called to give an account of our lives, and this anonymous letter serves even today as a daily examen for anyone who seriously claims the life of a Christian. Does this description of Christian life from the second century describe your new life in Christ today? Can you read about your

---

[278] From a letter to Diognetus, Office of Readings for Wednesday, Easter Week V, 840–842.

own saintly self in these words? If you can, then thank God and ask Him to preserve you. If not (or if not to the degree you wish), then the Lenten and Easter seasons are especially for you. Here are four ways that can make your future journeys into the Easter Mystery truly transformative not only for you, but also for the world.

1. Know where you are going.

We said at the outset that, like any expedition, a successful devotional journey into Easter requires that we know our destination. True, God and His Church guide us — blind, groping, and fallen creatures that we are — to our destination. Yet we are not forced to arrive at God's goal, any more than the members of the Chosen People were dragged along to the Promised Land. (After all, thanks to our fallen human nature, who among us, like the Israelites, has not wandered from the path — if not for forty years then at least momentarily?) Rather, we are meant to participate actively, consciously, and fully in our pilgrimage, and, as any intelligent traveler can attest, success is a matter of knowing the goal of the journey. In our case, that goal is the Paschal Mystery.

The Paschal Mystery is the suffering, death, Resurrection, and Ascension of Jesus, by which He set an eternal bridge between earth and heaven. Original sin, along with our subsequent personal sin, separates us from God's love. But God has made us for Himself, and He has taken the initiative in bringing us back. The Old Testament gave many peeks into this future restoration, especially the epic account of the Israelites' exodus out of Egypt. Yet, as great as the story is of Moses and his people — truly the stuff of Hollywood! — it is still only a shadow of what Jesus fulfills in His priestly bridge-building work on earth, and the same work that gains us access to the Church's sacraments and the Paschal Triduum.

Knowing our paschal goal — crossing from earth's sin to heaven's glory — makes all the difference in our devotional journey into the Easter Mystery. The liturgy's texts, signs, times, places, and actions all stand out in greater beauty and clarity when we see them in the light of the Paschal Mystery. So, as a part of your preparation for the next devotional journey, recall as clearly as you can the purpose of it all. In fact, as a further exercise that will fine-tune your spiritual GPS, explain the Paschal Mystery to another person. For laity, this can mean sitting down with your child, grandchild, spouse, friend, or classmate. For the clergy, this can mean unpacking this same mystery to parishioners or seminarians — or even other clergy! In any case, tell your audience what the Paschal Mystery is, why it is necessary, how all of salvation history leads to it and from it, and how it is the only means to becoming fully alive.

2. See sacramentally.

The liturgy generally, including Lent and Easter liturgies, can be examined in a variety of ways. Its rituals can be viewed from the *historical* vantage, for example. A fourth-century Iberian nun named Egeria leaves an account of her travels to Jerusalem, during which she participated in the Holy Week liturgies. These accounts might fruitfully be compared with other celebrations throughout the centuries, and in their light we might compare these other accounts of Holy Week with Pope Pius XII's 1955 revisions of the Holy Week liturgies. Alternatively, we could view today's Holy Week liturgies through *legal* lenses, as when we determine the earliest legitimate time to begin the Vigil so that it takes place in the necessary darkness, or the canonical requirements for catechumens or candidates for reception into the Church, or the rubrical instructions about the specifics of the washing of the feet (e.g., one foot or both? of men and women? washed by priest alone?). Still again, we can uncover the riches of the Easter celebrations by way of the magnificent *art* it has produced, such as musical settings of the *Ubi caritas* or the many versions of the Pietà. Each of these perspectives on the liturgy—history, law, art—yields true insights to the Easter Mystery and can facilitate our participation in the liturgy. Yet there is one consideration that stands above all others: the sacramental perspective.

Our sacred liturgy effects many things and communicates on many levels, but before all else it is a *sacramental* thing. Jesus Christ, the "image of the invisible God" (Col. 1:15), is Himself a sacrament of God the Father: whoever has seen Jesus has seen the Father (John 14:9). But Christ's incarnate sacramentality continues today, long after His Ascension—every day, every hour, every moment, our Lord comes to us in the Church's seven sacraments, her many sacramentals, and the sacramental signs and symbols of her liturgy. Recall St. Leo the Great's maxim: "Our Redeemer's visible presence has passed into the sacraments."[279] To see these sacraments and sacramentals is to see Jesus—along with His Father and the Holy Spirit.

Consequently, the more our senses—seeing, hearing, smelling, tasting, and touching—become attuned to sacramental

---

[279] St. Leo the Great, Office of Readings for Friday, Easter Week VI, 937.

expression, the more they encounter Jesus. It is helpful to know liturgical history, necessary that we follow its laws, and rewarding that we appreciate its beauty: but it is *essential* that we participate sacramentally. For priests, deacons, and liturgical ministers, this means presenting the Easter liturgies as given by the ritual books, in light of the Church's Tradition, and accommodated, where permitted, to participants. When ministers don't allow the liturgy's signs and symbols to express the Easter Mystery as the Church desires, these signposts to the paschal bridge cease to manifest Christ and His saving Paschal Mystery. A deacon, priest, or bishop who is lazy or careless in his practice of the priestly art—for the liturgy is precisely what these ordained men have been trained to do and do well—shifts the focus in the liturgy from revealing Christ to revealing more about himself.

At the same time, and as these ordained ministers symbolize Christ to us, the liturgy's other participants need to sense sacramentally. Only then can our minds move from what is seen on the surface to its underlying spiritual substance—a *mystagogical* way of seeing. Recall how St. Ambrose instructed his own newly baptized about such sight: "Do not then believe only what the eyes of your body tell you.... What is not comprehended by the eyes but is seen by the mind and the soul is seen in a truer and deeper sense."[280] To see the Easter Mystery in its fullness requires sacramental and mystagogical senses. Transformative life to the full includes seeing beneath the surface. In short, to see the Easter Mystery is to see the big picture: the one beginning with our creation in the garden and ending in heaven, arising from the depths of hell and ending at the Father's right hand.

---

[280] St. Ambrose, Office of Readings for Tuesday of the Fifteenth Week in Ordinary Time, vol. III, 492.

3. Journey with others.

Another helpful part of journeying fruitfully into the Easter Mystery includes our traveling companions. God means for our journey to be a group activity, whether in our wandering through the wilderness, building the paschal bridge, or scaling heaven's heights. Who wants to travel alone, after all? And who desires to battle the Devil alone? Even Jesus had angels, saints, and companions to accompany Him. Recall how often the Lenten and Easter liturgies required us to rely upon others. The proclamation of the Passion on Palm Sunday and Good Friday includes many voices. Likewise, the Mass of the Lord's Supper is a collective invitation to join in the journey, as it includes offerings for the poor and bringing Communion to those unable to be present. These tasks are not accomplished by the pastor or the lone kindly soul in the parish but are meted out among the entire Mystical Body. Recall that other great moment of teamwork during the Good Friday intercessions when the deacon (or another minister) introduces the prayer, the priest concludes the prayer, and the assembly approves the prayer with its "Amen"—the body of petitions offered for all. Then there's that tremendous family reunion at the Easter Vigil when we recount our forebears, invoke the holy ones in the Litany of the Saints, and welcome new members of our human family into the Mystical Body. Salvation is a group activity, even while it requires an individual's acquiescence.

Therefore, when Lent comes around again, be determined: don't go it alone! Find others to travel with. Pray for one another. Read Sacred Scripture together. Discuss spiritual insights with each other. And don't forget the sacraments! The Easter Vigil's sacraments of initiation are the high point of the Easter Mystery, and the celebration of the sacraments enlivens the Church, Christ' Bride and Body. Appreciating the intimacy between the liturgy and ecclesiology, between the sacraments and the Church, between my faith and yours, will keep us in good company and keep our journey going in the right direction.

4. Live as if you mean it!

God created us in His image and after His likeness (Gen. 1:26–27). And we saw in our journey that the story of Easter, which is the story of Jesus' Paschal Mystery, begins at creation. Our first parents sinned by desiring this image and likeness in the wrong way and for the wrong reason — that is, not according to God's design — hence, their fall from grace. All of the Old Testament serves as a foreshadowing, a preparation for Christ's restoration of this divine image in man. All of the New Testament's sacraments apply His saving grace to us today in order that we may become ever more godlike, as the Trinity had intended for us from the start. God wants each and every one of us to be saints — in fact, He won't settle for anything less than our perfection.

In his short but joyful life, Pier Giorgio Frassati (1901–1925) embodied the divine restoration brought by Christ. He truly lived in Christ: fed by the Eucharist, serving the poor and the infirm in the streets of his hometown, Turin, Italy, and incarnating the beatitudes for all around him to witness.[281] Frassati was a man fully alive. An avid mountain climber, he took as his life's motto

---

[281] Pope John Paul II named Pier Giorgio Frassati the "man of the eight beatitudes."

Verso l'alto, "To the heights!" Surrounding himself with God in the heights of prayer, he nevertheless brought that celestial life back into the world, to help spark divine life below. In a letter to a friend, he speaks of being among the living (*hoi zōntes*, as Pope Benedict explained above):

> Every day I understand better what a grace it is to be Catholic. The poor people who have no faith are wretched: to live without any faith, without a heritage to defend, without upholding the truth in a continual battle, is not living but struggling to make ends meet. We should never struggle to make ends meet but rather live, because even amid disappointments we must remember that we are the only ones who possess the truth, we have a faith to uphold, a hope to attain: our [heavenly] homeland.... Ever onward for the triumph of Christ's reign in society.[282]

When next Lent comes your way, remember Frassati's words: climb to the heights of Easter's holy mountain so that you can descend again and begin living even now. God wants you fully alive; He wants you to be like Him—even today. And He gives us the means to transform this divine desire into a human reality. He pours grace, or "Christ life," into our souls. And like the deer that longs for running streams (Ps. 42:2), our souls are quenched by the Easter Mystery—as if we were drinking it through the proverbial firehose! With mouths and hearts open, we can battle for the great paschal bridge and climb that holy mountain. The result will be nothing less than life, joy, and holiness.

---

[282]Cristina Siccardi, *Pier Giorgio Frassati: A Hero for Our Times* (San Francisco: Ignatius Press, 2016), 66.

Appendices

A

Summary Guide to Participation

✠

How to Enter the Combat Stupendous: Ash Wednesday and Lent

The fundamental insight: God made man and woman in His image and according to His likeness. Original sin and personal sin kill the grace within and efface the beauty of God's image in us. Jesus' Paschal Mystery—His suffering, death, Resurrection, and Ascension—bridges the divide separating fallen earth from glorious heaven, and the Lenten and Easter liturgies are our ticket to pass over to heaven as restored, radiant, beautiful creatures.

The principal activity: Know where Lent is leading—from the dust and ashes of earth to the restored life, joy, and holiness in God. Our devotional journey to divine restoration passes over Jesus' great bridge. Explain the Paschal Mystery—what it is, why it is necessary, and what it does—to another person. Listen carefully to the liturgy's readings and prayers, and look incisively at its many unique rites for the Passover.

How to Battle for the Paschal Mystery: Palm Sunday and Holy Week

The fundamental insight: Jesus Christ won salvation for the world and glory for God by His Paschal Mystery. The liturgies of Holy Week manifest and communicate this mystery in the world today, and Jesus continues to work as Prime Minister. As Jesus was accompanied by angels and saints during His paschal work two thousand years ago, so are we accompanied today. Since Christ prayed and fasted in history's saving act, we do likewise now. Because Jesus manifested divine life and victory through particular, concrete signs and actions, we rely on His saving sacraments and sacramentals to struggle for the paschal bridge.

The principal activity: Keep your eyes fixed upon Christ by erecting seasonal images of Him at home, school, or work. Consciously invoke your personal patron saint and your guardian angel. Exercise penitential practices, such as almsgiving, fasting, reading Scripture, or praying parts of the Liturgy of the Hours, to a greater degree during Lent. Receive the sacrament of penance frequently, and attend Mass as often as possible during the week. These God-given weapons will help you to win Lent's battles.

How to Obey Orders: Holy Thursday's *Mandatum*

The fundamental insight: The liturgies and sacraments of the Paschal Triduum—from Thursday evening's Mass of the Lord's Supper until Easter Sunday's Evening Prayer—present Christ and His saving work to a superlative degree. The mystery of Christ present in his Mystical Body, the Church, appears in the *mandatum*, His command of brotherly love. We respond to Jesus' command by the washing of the feet, the presentation of gifts for the poor, and the bringing of the Eucharist to the homebound.

The principal activity: Be aware of your sacramental surroundings as Holy Thursday approaches—growing sunlight, increasing warmth, earth's new life—for each reveal Christ and His salvation. Know that His salvation includes our participation and that we are called to serve others in His name, not only within the liturgy of the Lord's Supper, but outside of the Mass as well. Find particular ways to answer His call to love and serve others.

How to Do This: Holy Thursday's Eucharist and Priesthood

The fundamental insight: Jesus fulfills the Lord's prescriptions to Moses and the people in the Land of Egypt prior to their exodus. But more than looking back into history, Holy Thursday commands the future Church to celebrate Christ's Good Friday sacrifice under the forms of bread and wine. Through sacramental ordination, Christ bestows on His priests the power to consecrate bread and wine and make His entire Paschal Mystery present. For their part, the lay faithful share in Jesus' priesthood through baptism and are empowered to join their whole selves to Jesus' gift to the Father through the hands of the priest.

The principal activity: Along with the Eucharist, the priesthood is born on Holy Thursday, so pray at this time for priests. Consider attending Holy Week's Chrism Mass, where, apart from the blessing of the Holy Oils, priests renew their priestly promises and the faithful intercede to God for them. Meditate on the Lord's instructions to the Chosen People as heard in the First Reading for the Mass of the Lord's Supper. After the Mass, spend time adoring the Eucharist, considering Jesus' words at the Last Supper as recorded in the Gospel of John, chapters 13–17.

How to Intercede for the World:
Good Friday's Cross

The fundamental insight: Good Friday stands at the center of the Paschal Triduum, extending the Cross's arms back to Holy Thursday and ahead to the Easter Vigil. The Good Friday liturgy recalls Christ's work on this day by recounting His Passion and Cross, the birth of His Bride, the Church, from His opened side, and His priestly intercession for the salvation of the whole world. These mysteries are sacramentalized in the liturgy's readings, especially the Passion from St. John, the adoration of the cross, and the expanded Universal Prayer.

The principal activity: We heard the Passion of Christ on Palm Sunday from either St. Matthew, St. Mark, or St. Luke. Today, as we hear it read from St. John's perspective, listen closely to the details, placing yourself among these in your mind's eye. See in the wood of the cross the material out of which Jesus, the Pontifex Maximus, builds the bridge to heaven. Focus on His opened side and reflect how His life-giving water and blood became His Bride's body, who is our supernatural mother. As Jesus died for all, pray intently during the Universal Prayer for the many categories of people, applying His channels of grace to those in your life who need His divine assistance.

How to Go to Hell—and Come Back Alive: Holy Saturday's Silence

The fundamental insight: While Jesus' body lies in the tomb on Holy Saturday, His divine person harrows hell, preaching the Good News even to the dead, and leads the righteous out of death's grasp. Until He returns, the Church and her children wait in silence, by fasting, and with prayer.

The principal activity: Meditate upon an image of Christ crucified or lying in the tomb (e.g., by Hans Holbein), or His descent into hell, or of his Sorrowful Mother. Surround yourself with silence. Prayer and fasting are especially efficacious during this day. Pray the Office of Readings or Morning Prayer with the rest of the Church.

How to Enter the Promised Land: The Easter Vigil's *Lucernarium* and Liturgy of the Word

The fundamental insight: In this Age of the Church, Jesus manifests and communicates His saving grace through sacraments and sacramental signs. The Easter Vigil's blessing of fire, preparation of the candle, and procession into the church building present to our senses Christ's Passover from death to life. The poetic *Exsultet* proclaims to our ears our happy fault that has won, by the Trinity's unfathomable plan, our salvation. The Liturgy of the Word announces to meditative minds and hearts God's preparation for Jesus' Paschal Mystery — and ours — throughout the ages.

The principal activity: Enter the celebration with eyes wide open, for its multilayered liturgical signs and symbols present the victorious Christ to our senses. Take in every detail surrounding the fire's blessing, the candle's preparation, and the procession's movement. Notice and reflect on the *Exsultet*'s symbols. See yourself in the many readings: formed by the Father's hands from the earth's clay, accompanying Abraham and Isaac to Mount Moriah, and traveling with the Chosen People through the Red Sea. Then share your insights with others during Easter Sunday and the entire Easter Octave, for a spectacle such as the Vigil should make a long-lasting impression.

How to Be Re-Created: The Easter Vigil's Sacraments

The fundamental insight: The Church's seven sacra-ments—the first three of which are celebrated at the Easter Vigil—are the superlative means by which fallen men and women are conformed to the living God. Baptism gives birth to new life, confirmation intensifies that same life, the Eucharist nourishes that new life. By opening the paschal bridge before us, the sacraments make us divine, which was God's plan from the beginning.

The principal activity: With sacramental senses attuned to new life, pray for and participate with those about to be baptized, supporting their supernatural death and resurrection in baptism's waters, even as you recall your own baptism. Like Mary and the Apostles in the Upper Room, pray for the intense outpouring of the Holy Spirit upon the initiates and upon the whole Church, confirm-ing what has already occurred at baptism. Receive Com-munion as if for the first time, tasting in this fruit of the tree of the Cross the fare of heaven's wedding banquet. As any child resembles his parents, know that the new children of God are called to participate in the Father's divine life even now, and that the sacraments are the God-given means to make our transformation possible. Do not receive God's grace in vain (2 Cor. 6:1)!

How to Become God: The Easter Season and Pentecost

The fundamental insight: We were made to participate in God's divine life, to radiate His image and likeness. God the Father sends His Son to make us His adopted brothers and sisters: "Since it was the will of God's only-begotten Son that men should share in his divinity, he assumed our nature in order that by becoming man he might make men gods" (St. Thomas Aquinas). Jesus works principally through the sacraments, along with Sacred Scripture, and does so with the Holy Spirit, His cooperator, who amplifies and animates the divine life within us.

The principal activity: Answer the call from God and for God—to become God! Know that you were born from the heart of the Trinity and destined to abide in the midst of the Trinity. Grow your divine life by receiving the sacraments, through prayer, and by doing good works. As a family or with another group, imitate the prayerful apostles and Mother of God, who awaited the special outpouring of the Holy Spirit. Consider praying a novena to the Holy Spirit.

B

Glossary of Terms

✠

Age of the Church: The present period of salvation history occurring after the descent of the Holy Spirit at Pentecost and before Christ's Second Coming. In this age, "Christ now lives and acts in and with his Church, in a new way appropriate to this new age. He acts through the sacraments" (CCC 1076) (see chapter 2).

Anamnesis: The religious act of remembering that not only recalls a past event but in some way renders that event and its effects present today. The Chosen People *remembered* their initial Passover in this manner, and Jesus tells His apostles at the Last Supper to "do this in *remembrance* of me," that is, as an *anamnesis*. Thus, when the Church remembers Christ's Paschal Mystery, its reality and fruits are made present (see chapter 4).

Hylomorphic: At its most basic level, wood (*hyle*) that is given form (*morphe*). Aristotle, for example, used the term to express any being composed of matter and form. St. Thomas Aquinas applied the term to the Church's sacraments, themselves composites of matter (e.g., water, oil, bread) and words (e.g., "I baptize you …"; "Be sealed with the Gift of the Holy Spirit"; "This is my body") (see chapter 5).

Lucernarium: The first of the Easter Vigil's four main parts, consisting of the elements up to the Liturgy of the Word: the blessing of the fire, the preparation of the Easter candle, the procession into the Church, and the singing of the *Exsultet* (see chapter 7).

Mystagogical catechesis, or mystagogy: A form of liturgical catechesis that leads participants from what can be detected outwardly by the senses (e.g., a candle, incense, the *Exsultet*) to the spiritual reality within, who is ultimately Jesus. As the *Catechism of the Catholic Church* describes it, mystagogical catechesis "aims to initiate people into the mystery of Christ (It is 'mystagogy') by proceeding from the visible to the invisible, from the sign to the thing signified, from the 'sacraments' to the 'mysteries'" (1075) (see the introduction).

Original sin: Adam and Eve's first disobedience of God's Word, by which they chose to follow their own plan and path to glory rather than God's plan for them. Their fall from grace caused death and destruction for themselves and the rest of the world and marred the divine likeness in them. By the choice for God the Father, Christ, the Second Adam, would restore grace and eternal life to the world (see chapter 1).

Paschal Mystery: "Christ's work of redemption accomplished principally by his Passion, death, Resurrection, and glorious Ascension," by which he *passed* from the fallen world of sin to the heavenly world of the Father. These four distinct elements—suffering, death, resurrection, ascension—are the substantial reality standing beneath each of Easter's sacramental signs and symbols. They are called "paschal" because they form a bridge by which Jesus and those who belong to Him cross over—that is, pass over—to a new heaven and a new earth (see chapter 1).

Penance: Interior penance is the conversion of the heart away from sin and to God, a turn that is expressed outwardly by penitential actions, the chief among them being fasting, prayer, and giving alms (see CCC 1430–1439). The sacrament of penance includes the penitent's contrition, confession to a priest, and satisfaction, and it bestows God's forgiveness (see chapter 2).

Pontifex: *Pontifex* means "bridge builder" and is one of the names for priest, since the priest mediates between God and man, thus bridging the separation between them. Jesus, since He is the greatest builder of all times, is called the *Pontifex Maximus* (see chapter 1).

Sacrament: An efficacious sign of grace, "instituted by Christ and entrusted to his Church, by which divine life is dispensed to us" through the work of the Holy Spirit (CCC 1131, glossary). The person and saving work of Christ are presented to us today in a privileged way by means of the sacraments: "What was visible in our Savior," St. Leo the Great teaches, "has passed over into his sacraments" (see chapter 8).

Sacramental character: An indelible mark or seal given by the sacraments of baptism, confirmation, and holy orders that conforms the recipient to Jesus and enables him or her to exercise Christ's priestly, prophetic, and kingly offices (see chapter 4).

Sacramental principle: The means by which God encounters us, and we encounter God, through the medium of sensible signs and symbols (see chapters 2, 7).

Sacrifice: In the Christian tradition, sacrifice is the giving to God one's very heart and will, those things that God will only receive but is powerless to take. Jesus' sacrifice was acceptable to the Father since it signified His complete and loving obedience to the Father's will, despite His great suffering and death (see chapter 5).

Theosis: Also called *divinization*, the process by which God's grace transforms His creation, chiefly man, into sharers of His divine life. As St. Athanasius describes it, "the Son of God be-came man so that we might become God" (chapter 8).

Triduum: Literally "three days," this shortest of the Church's liturgical seasons begins with the Mass of the Lord's Supper on Holy Thursday evening and concludes with Vespers (Evening Prayer) on Easter Sunday (see the introduction and chapter 3).

Typology: One of the Church's three spiritual senses of Sacred Scripture, in which persons or events of the Old Testament pre-figure or foreshadow (that is, are "types" of) Christ, His Church, and His sacraments. The exodus of the Chosen People from Egypt to freedom, for example, is a type of Passover that Jesus would fulfill and establish in a definitive way (see CCC 115–117) (see chapters 8, 9).

C

Recommended Reading

✠

Bouyer, Louis. *The Paschal Mystery: Meditations on the Liturgy of the Last Three Days of Holy Week*. Chicago: Regnery, 1950.

Congregation for Divine Worship and the Discipline of the Sacraments. Circular Letter on the Preparation and Celebration of the Easter Feasts *Paschalis Sollemnitatis* (January 16, 1988).

Gaillard, Jean. *Holy Week and Easter: A Liturgical Commentary*. Collegeville, MN: Liturgical Press, 1954.

Ratzinger, Joseph. *Jesus of Nazareth, Holy Week: From the Entrance into Jerusalem to the Resurrection*. San Francisco: Ignatius Press, 2011.

———. *Journey to Easter: Spiritual Reflections for the Lenten Season*. New York: Crossroad, 2006.

Turner, Paul. *Glory in the Cross: Holy Week in the Third Edition of The Roman Missal*. Collegeville, MN: Liturgical Press, 2011.

Yarnold, Edward. *The Awe-Inspiring Rites of Initiation: The Origins of the R.C.I.A.* Collegeville, MN: Liturgical Press, 1994.

Biographical Note

---✛---

Christopher Carstens is Director of the Office for Sacred Worship in the Diocese of La Crosse, Wisconsin, a visiting faculty member at the Liturgical Institute at the University of St. Mary of the Lake in Mundelein, Illinois, and editor of the *Adoremus Bulletin*. He is author of *A Devotional Journey into the Mass* (Sophia) and, along with Father Douglas Martis, the coauthor of *Mystical Body, Mystical Voice: Encountering Christ in the Words of the Mass* (Liturgy Training Publications). He lives in Soldiers Grove, Wisconsin, with his wife and eight children.

SPIRITUAL DIRECTION
☙ SERIES ❧

SOPHIA INSTITUTE PRESS

If this book has caused a stir in your heart to continue to pursue your relationship with God, we invite you to explore two extraordinary resources, SpiritualDirection.com and the Avila Institute for Spiritual Formation.

The readers of SpiritualDirection.com reside in almost every country of the world where hearts yearn for God. It is the world's most popular English site dedicated to authentic Catholic spirituality.

The students of the Avila Institute for Spiritual Formation sit at the feet of the rich and deep well of the wisdom of the saints.

You can find more about the Avila Institute at
WWW.AVILA-INSTITUTE.COM.

Sophia Institute

Sophia Institute is a nonprofit institution that seeks to nurture the spiritual, moral, and cultural life of souls and to spread the Gospel of Christ in conformity with the authentic teachings of the Roman Catholic Church.

Sophia Institute Press fulfills this mission by offering translations, reprints, and new publications that afford readers a rich source of the enduring wisdom of mankind.

Sophia Institute also operates the popular online resource CatholicExchange.com. *Catholic Exchange* provides world news from a Catholic perspective as well as daily devotionals and articles that will help readers to grow in holiness and live a life consistent with the teachings of the Church.

In 2013, Sophia Institute launched Sophia Institute for Teachers to renew and rebuild Catholic culture through service to Catholic education. With the goal of nurturing the spiritual, moral, and cultural life of souls, and an abiding respect for the role and work of teachers, we strive to provide materials and programs that are at once enlightening to the mind and ennobling to the heart; faithful and complete, as well as useful and practical.

Sophia Institute gratefully recognizes the Solidarity Association for preserving and encouraging the growth of our apostolate over the course of many years. Without their generous and timely support, this book would not be in your hands.

www.SophiaInstitute.com
www.CatholicExchange.com
www.SophiaInstituteforTeachers.org

Sophia Institute Press® is a registered trademark of Sophia Institute. Sophia Institute is a tax-exempt institution as defined by the Internal Revenue Code, Section 501(c)(3). Tax ID 22-2548708.